SMART BREAKOUT TRADING

A Data-Driven Blueprint For High-Probability Breakout Trade

Tom Anderton

TABLE OF CONTENTS

INTRODUCTION

I'm not sure what brought you to this book, or in what state of mind you find yourself as you open these first pages.

Maybe you're a trader who has just stepped into the market—looking for a method that feels simple and clear, because somewhere along the way you've heard someone say, "Good trading should be simple."

Or maybe you've been in this game for a while. You've seen how unforgiving the market can be—how it lifts you up one moment and crushes you the next. You've been through cycles of excitement and frustration, moments when you felt worn out but never completely gave up. Deep down, you're still searching for a way to trade that truly makes sense, something solid enough to rely on for years to come.

It's also possible that you've read plenty of trading books, learned dozens of strategies, and yet none of them have left a real mark on you—none that made you stop and say, "This is it. This is what I've been looking for all along."

However you've come to this book, I believe it's not by accident. The fact that you're here, reading these lines, already tells me there's a quiet connection between you and me.

And there's nothing I'd appreciate more than if you stay with me until the very last page—long enough to feel something click inside you. So that by the end, whether you're just beginning or already a trader with years behind you, you'll close this book feeling both inspired and grounded—your passion burning strong, your mind steady and cool.

That's been my only wish since I started typing the very first words of this book—a collection of lessons and reflections from fifteen years in the market. Trading has become an inseparable part of my life: deeply engaging, but never something I let rush or overwhelm me.

Like many traders, I began with indicators on my chart. To be fair, there were times when they worked well enough, giving me results that made me believe trading could be easy. However, things started falling apart when I increased my capital, broke my own risk management rules, and those same indicators suddenly ceased to make sense. It all seemed to collapse at once—and I couldn't understand why.

Later on, I took a step back and began observing the market more deeply, not to become some kind of trading guru, but to find a mental foundation—something that could support every trading approach I would explore afterward. From there, I wanted to relearn trading from the ground up.

Out of that reflection, I realized there were two essential elements.

- First: The foundation — the battle between the Bulls and the Bears. Nothing else. No indicators. No magical formula.

From that moment on, my perspective on price charts underwent a complete transformation. Every candlestick started to feel like a frame in an action movie, where two forces were constantly fighting for control—the Bulls pushing the price upward, and the Bears trying to drag it down. Each price zone was like a battlefield.

I began to understand why the price paused, why it bounced, why it was rejected, and why it broke through. The market started to make sense—it became structured, no longer a random storm of candles and lines. Even then, I still didn't have a clear, actionable strategy, but for the first time, I could *see* the logic behind what was happening.

That was when I realized I had only understood the market on a very basic level. Knowing what was happening wasn't enough; I still needed a way to turn that understanding into consistent profit. And that led me to the second key element:

- Second: A trading approach that is simple enough, yet broad enough to cover the whole market — built upon the ongoing battle between the Bulls and the Bears: **Breakout Trading**.

After testing many different Price Action methods, breakout trading was the only one that truly made sense to me — the only approach that felt logical, clear, and consistent. It wasn't just about drawing patterns and waiting for the price to break. Breakout trading, to me, was a complete process: observing the market, studying price behavior, analyzing the balance of power, and finally identifying entry points through a set of rules that had been proven over thousands of trades.

That's why, for me, breakout is not just a *setup* — it's a mindset.

When you've spent enough time in the market and lived through enough trades, you eventually come to recognize these two timeless components. Once you do, trading starts to feel exactly as it should be — boring but effective.

The unfortunate truth is that most traders never realize this. They spend their time chasing something *better*, *newer*, or *more complicated.*

That very tendency became my biggest motivation to finish this book — a book simple enough for new traders to grasp and apply for the long run, yet professional and profound enough for experienced traders to find real value in, the kind that few trading books ever manage to deliver.

In this book, we'll walk step by step through the process of building a trading strategy with a high probability of success. Throughout this journey, the constant battle between the Bulls and the Bears will serve as the thread that ties everything together — shaping every trading mindset, every strategy, and every tactic you'll learn. As you move through the chapters, you may find the ideas both familiar and new at the same time. But once all of them come together into a complete trading system, you'll feel that natural urge to start trading right away — not out of excitement, but because of how practical and grounded it feels.

Don't worry — I won't let you run ahead of yourself and stumble the way you might have with other strategies in the past.

In this book, I'll lay out a roadmap to help you bring theory into real trading practice — effectively and with purpose. Along the way, I'll point out the mental and psychological traps that traders often fall into. I'll help you avoid those potholes by guiding you along paths that may at first seem longer, yet in truth will shorten your journey in this profession more than you could imagine.

That's what makes this book unique: the part I value most isn't just the trading strategies themselves, but something far more important that underlies them.

Here, I share ideas and insights that are both new and familiar — not only about trading, but also about the universal principles of success in any field. I want you to believe that earning sustainable profits in this market is absolutely possible — and that *you* can be one of the traders who make it happen. That belief, and the desire to help you reach it, has been my greatest motivation in completing this book.

I hope that, by now, you've begun to feel a sense of connection — a quiet resonance — before we step together into the next chapters of this journey, about the laws of the Bulls and the Bears, the thread that will weave through every idea and concept that follows.

Now then, let's begin Chapter 1: The Law of Bulls and Bears — where it all begins.

CHAPTER 1: THE LAW OF BULLS AND BEARS

If we were to think of the market as a game, it would resemble a tug-of-war more than anything else. Two teams stand at opposite ends of the rope, pouring all their strength into pulling it toward their side. Each time one side gains ground, the other immediately fights back. The rope tightens, trembles, and sways back and forth without rest. At moments, it seems one side has finally won—but just one short breath later, the balance shifts again.

That is the true nature of the market. Every single candle you see on a chart is the result of millions of buying and selling actions—of pushing and pulling, of belief and fear. On one side stand the Bulls, those who believe prices will continue to rise; on the other, the Bears, who bet that prices will fall. These two forces constantly take turns holding control, creating the rhythm of the market—sometimes strong, sometimes weak—just like the rope in a tug-of-war: always tense, always in motion.

The Law of Bulls and Bears: The Never-Ending Battle

At the world's most famous financial center — Wall Street — the bronze statue of a bull, its horns thrusting upward, has long stood as a symbol of confidence, optimism, and rising prices. The Bull, when attacking, drives its horns upward — a powerful motion that represents the act of pushing prices higher, the force of buyers. In contrast, the Bear attacks by striking downward with its front paws, symbolizing the push to drive prices lower — the force of sellers.

From that image, people have come to see the market as a vast arena, where every second, every minute, a series of upward charges and downward strikes takes place.

In this book, the concept of the *Law of Bulls and Bears* is not merely a metaphor. It is a principle — a way of understanding how price truly moves, defined by the shifting balance of power between buyers and sellers. Whether you trade forex, stocks, commodities, or crypto, the deeper nature of the market remains the same, revolving around just two fundamental actions: buying and selling.

Even in everyday life, this law is always around us — from the price of groceries at the supermarket to the cost of housing or gold. Everything moves according to the same principle of supply and demand: when demand increases, prices tend to rise; when supply exceeds demand, prices naturally fall. In the financial markets, this mechanism is reflected vividly in every candlestick, in every movement you see on a price chart.

What's fascinating is that once you truly understand the *Law of Bulls and Bears*, you can explain almost every price phenomenon without memorizing a long list of patterns or complex concepts. Candlestick formations, market structures, and trend theories — all of them stem from this simple dynamic of buying and selling.

When you grasp how these two forces operate, you begin to see the market differently. You can tell when buying pressure is dominant, when sellers are taking control, and, more importantly, when the timing is right to enter or exit a trade.

Imagine the market as a world divided into two kingdoms — the Kingdom of Bulls and the Kingdom of Bears. The Kingdom of Bears lies above, representing the area where sellers hold control. The Kingdom of Bulls lies below, representing the zone dominated by buyers. Between these two realms lies a constantly shifting border — a battlefield where endless clashes take place, each side striving to seize the other's territory.

In every battle, both sides rely on two key elements: *offensive power* and *territory*.

The *offensive power* represents immediate strength — it could be a surge in trading volume or a strong candlestick moving in the dominant direction.

The *territory*, on the other hand, is where each side gathers its strength and prepares for the subsequent counterattack — much like key price zones on a chart. In these areas, prices often return to retest before continuing their move.

Once you understand these two elements, you begin to see how the market truly operates. Price movements no longer appear random, but rather as a series of tactical and strategic exchanges — a constant battle for every inch of price territory. And this is where the deeper exploration begins — the journey into the Law of Bulls and Bears, the fundamental law behind every market movement.

Offensive Power

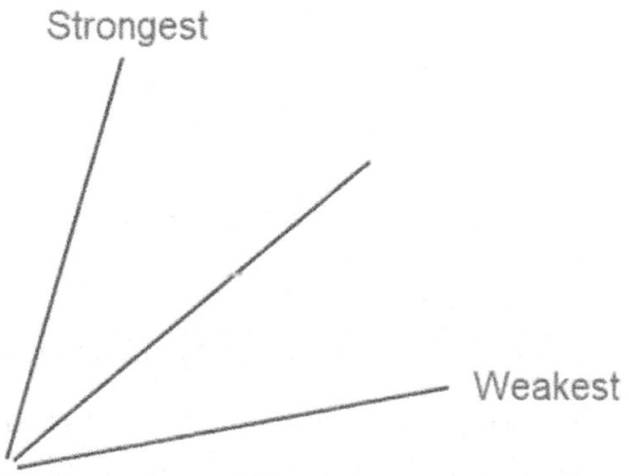

Figure 1.1: Offensive Power

When we talk about the battle between the Bulls and the Bears, the first thing we need to understand is power — the strength of each side during a price movement. The key question is: how can we tell which side is stronger and which is weaker? If we only look at candlesticks, it's not easy to see, because a chart often shows movement, but not necessarily which side is in control.

There's a simple way to identify the balance of power between the two sides — by observing the slope of price movement. When the price moves upward or downward with a steeper slope, it shows that the offensive power of the leading side is stronger. Conversely, when the slope starts to flatten and price slows down, it signals that side is losing strength.

You can imagine this through three different slopes: one gentle, one moderate, and one steep. The steeper the slope, the greater the power. The flatter the slope, the weaker the push.

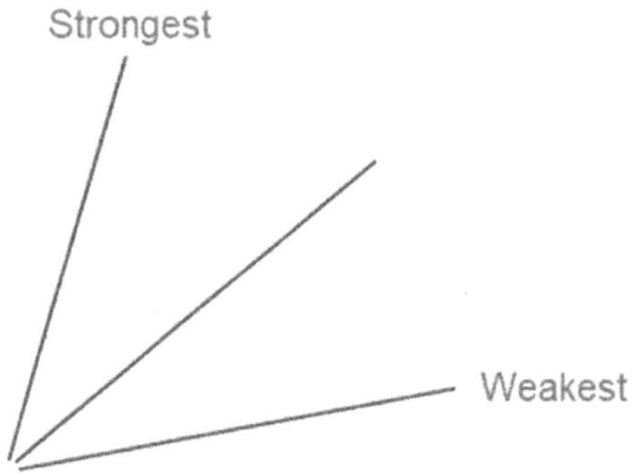

Figure 1.1: Offensive Power

By looking at the slope of price movement, we can clearly see the offensive power of each side and recognize when the market is accelerating or slowing down. It is the very first step in understanding how the market moves under the Law of Bulls and Bears.

When buyers are strong, the upward push becomes more pronounced, and as a result, the slope of price movement grows steeper. However, suppose after a sharp rally, the sellers are still able to drive the price back down. In that case, it means their selling power must be significantly stronger. In other words, to reverse a steep bullish move, the Bears must gather enough strength to overcome the prior buying force.

Conversely, when buying power is weaker, price tends to rise more slowly, forming a gentler slope. In such situations, if sellers step in, they do not need much effort to turn the market around. Even a moderate wave of selling pressure can be enough to stop and reverse a weak uptrend.

Territory

While offensive power shows how aggressively each side attacks, the territory is where that side consolidates and defends its position. On a price chart, the territories of buyers and sellers are usually represented by key price zones — areas where both forces frequently gather strength to defend or launch counterattacks. These zones are known as Bull Territories and Bear Territories.

Let's start with the Bull Territory, also known as the buyers' defense zone. This is the area where, in the past, strong buying pressure pushed prices sharply higher. For that reason, when price returns to this zone, buyers often re-enter the market, creating fresh upward pressure that causes price to bounce and prevents it from falling further.

Simply put, the Bull Territory is where buyers tend to react most strongly in defense of their positions. The strength of this zone depends on the steepness of the prior bullish move: the steeper the move, the stronger the buying power, and the more capable the Bull Territory is of holding price. Conversely, if the preceding rally was weak and shallow, the Bull Territory formed from it will be less effective at halting a decline.

The same principle applies to the Bears. Their territory, also known as the sellers' defense zone, is the area where strong selling pressure previously drove prices down sharply. When price rises back into this zone, sellers often rejoin the battle, applying downward pressure that pushes the market lower and prevents it from breaking above resistance. The Bear Territory, therefore, serves as the defensive line where sellers protect the ground they have established or reclaimed. Just like with the Bulls, the strength of a Bear Territory depends on the steepness of the prior bearish move: the sharper the drop, the stronger the selling power, and the more effectively the Bear Territory can stop an upward advance.

Notes: The concepts and principles discussed in this book apply equally to both sides of the market — uptrends and downtrends. To avoid unnecessary repetition, most of the illustrations and examples will be presented in the context of an uptrend. The entire logic remains symmetrical in a downtrend, with the only difference being the direction of price movement.

Types of Bull Zones

In practice, we can encounter several types of Bull zones, depending on how the price moves and how buying power emerges within those areas. Below are the common types of Bull zones found in the market.

Bull Zone at Market Bottoms

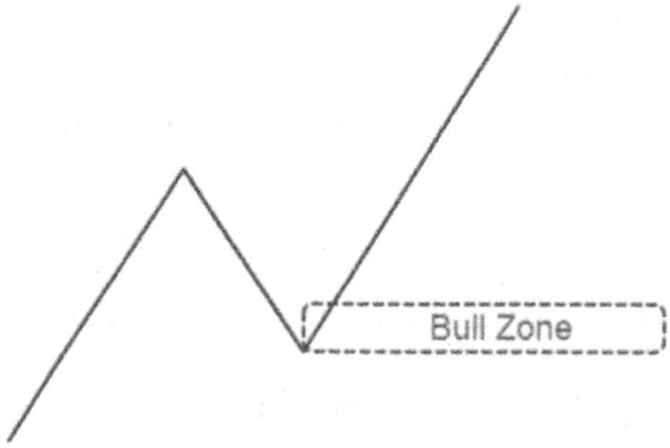

Figure 1.2: Bull Zone

The most familiar type of Bull zone is the one that forms at key market bottoms. This is where the Bears have weakened after a period of attack, and the Bulls begin to regain control. In other words, it marks the moment when strength shifts from sellers to buyers — the turning point at which a new upward force begins to form, countering the previous trend.

In this area, for the price to reverse and start rising, the Bulls need strong upward momentum. That very momentum creates the Bull zone. Later, when the price returns to retest this bottom area, buyers tend to step in aggressively, pushing the price upward again. The more clearly defined the bottom — meaning price has reacted strongly there in the past or formed a distinct reversal pattern — the stronger the corresponding Bull zone will be.

Bull Zone as the Start of Strong Price Momentum

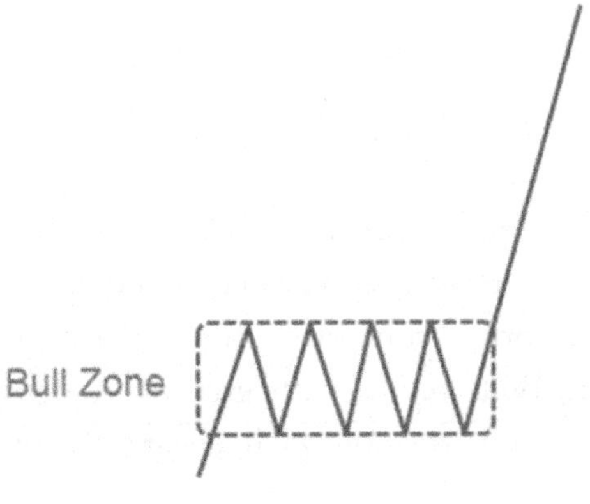

Figure 1.3: Bull Zone

A Bull zone can also form in areas where a strong upward momentum begins — the very starting point of a powerful price move. This is often where the market has just gone through a period of tug-of-war between buyers and sellers, before the Bulls gain the upper hand and create a strong push that drives price sharply higher.

When price breaks out of this zone of conflict, it leaves behind an important trace — the Bull zone itself. Later, when price returns to retest this area, buying pressure often reappears, helping the market recover and continue its upward trend.

Bull Zone at Broken Previous Highs

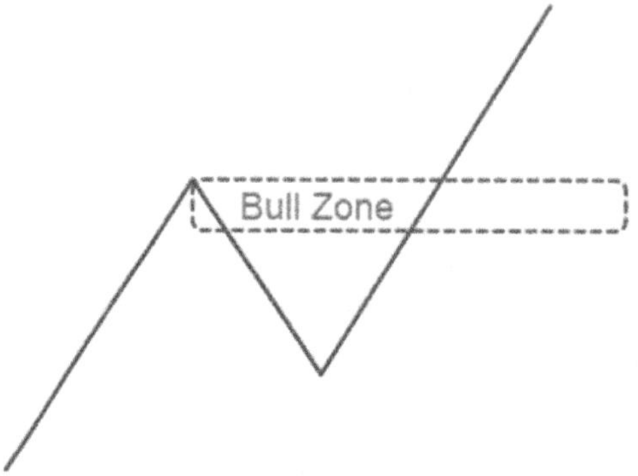

Figure 1.4: Bull Zone

A Bull zone can also form at a previous high that has been broken. This is the area where, in the past, the Bears once held control, creating enough pressure to stop the price from rising further and push it downward. However, when the Bulls return with greater strength and succeed in driving the price above that previous high, it signals a complete shift in the balance of power.

Breaking through a previous high means that the Bulls have overpowered the earlier selling pressure — and to achieve that, they must possess significant offensive power. Once that resistance is broken, the old high transforms into a new support area — in other words, it becomes a Bull zone. When price later returns to retest this area, buyers often re-enter the market, creating the classic upward rebound reaction.

The Attack and Occupation of the Opponent's Territory

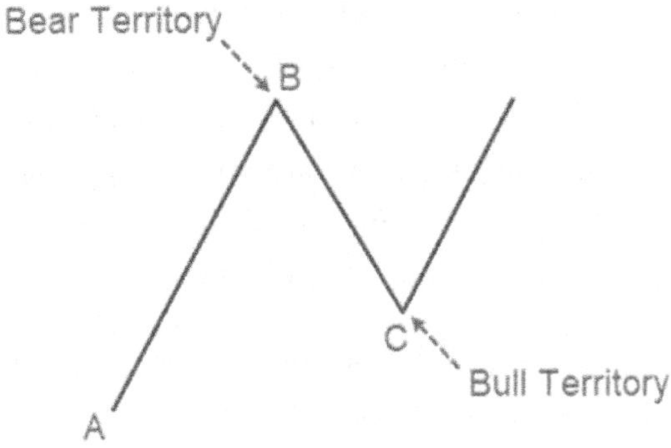

Figure 1.5: The Attacks

Now, let's take the perspective of a Bull offensive and observe how the Bears resist, creating the price movements we see on the chart. In reality, every fluctuation in the market is the result of this constant tug-of-war between the two sides — one attempting to expand its territory, the other defending or reclaiming the ground it has lost.

Suppose the Bulls are in a position of strength. They launch an attack and push the price from point A to point B. This marks a phase where buying power dominates, as indicated by a clear upward movement in prices. However, once the price reaches area B, the Bears begin their counterattack. If their offensive power at that moment exceeds that of the Bulls, they will drive the price back down toward area C. As a result, area B — where the counterattack began — becomes the new territory of the Bears.

The strength of this Bear territory depends on the selling power at that moment. If the selling pressure is strong, we will see a steep decline, showing that the Bears are in full control of the situation. Conversely, if the decline is shallow and slow, it indicates weak resistance, meaning the Bear territory formed there is fragile and unlikely to hold for long.

Because the Bulls had launched a strong attack earlier, once the Bears push the price down to a certain level, the Bulls will soon counterattack. That area becomes the Bulls' territory, often aligning with previous lows from which the price once rebounded sharply. In this case, point C represents the Bulls' territory. When the price moves into area C, buyers begin to re-enter the market. This suggests there are still a large number of pending buy orders in that zone, reflecting the Bulls' confidence that this is a valuable area to defend or expand their positions.

When the Bulls push the price from area C back up toward the Bears' territory at B, two possible scenarios can unfold.

Scenario 1

The first scenario is when the Bulls are stronger than the Bears. In this case, the buying pressure is strong enough to completely break through the territory that the Bears had previously established. Price moves above area B and closes firmly above it, marking the Bulls' successful occupation of the Bears' territory.

This signifies that control over the price zone at B has officially shifted to the Bulls. From that moment on, area B — which once acted as resistance — now becomes a new support zone for the Bulls.

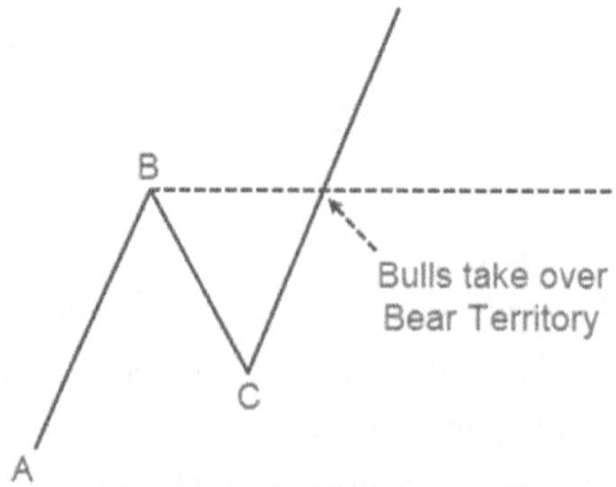

Figure 1.6: Territory Flip

After the Bulls capture the Bears' territory at area B, if the Bears launch a counterattack and push the price back into that region, the situation changes once again. At this point, the Bulls will usually step in to defend the position they have just gained. If their buying power is strong enough, they can drive the price upward again from that area.

However, there is one important point to note: the territory the Bulls have just taken at B is usually weaker than their original territory, area C, where the initial attack began. Area C had been reinforced by stronger buying power and a larger volume of orders, while area B is a newly conquered zone, gained after a period of conflict.

Scenario 2

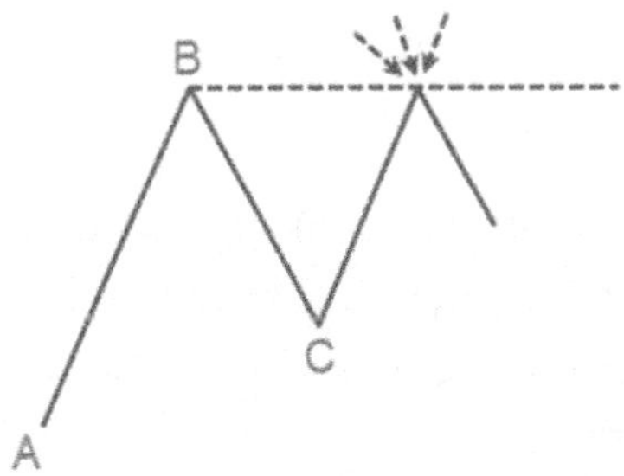

Figure 1.7: Territory Defended

In the second scenario, the Bulls launch an attack on the Bears' territory at area B, but this time the Bears are stronger. Instead of allowing the Bulls to break through their defense, the Bears quickly counterattack, pushing the price back down and maintaining control over area B.

At this stage, two territories are clearly defined: area C belongs to the Bulls, and area B belongs to the Bears. When the price drops toward the lower region, the Bulls attempt to defend their territory by pushing the price upward. Conversely, when the price moves toward the upper region, the Bears counter with selling pressure to drive it back down.

When both sides operate within the range between these two territories and neither is strong enough to overpower the other, the market enters a temporary state of balance. During this phase, the price typically fluctuates within a defined range, forming a sideways pattern. This tug-of-war continues until one side gathers enough strength to break through either the upper or lower boundary. When that happens, the market reveals which side has gained superiority, and the next direction of price becomes clear.

Another important note concerns the various levels of attack. Just as in the military, forces are divided into various ranks and scales — from platoons and companies to battalions — the same applies to the market. The battles between the Bulls and Bears occur across multiple levels, corresponding to different timeframes on the chart. Smaller offensives on lower timeframes form the foundation of larger offensives on higher ones. In turn, the larger movements on higher timeframes influence and shape the smaller battles occurring below them. Each timeframe is therefore interconnected, like layers within a well-structured military system.

For example, a successful Bull offensive on a higher timeframe is often the result of a series of smaller victories on lower timeframes. At the same time, that offensive may itself be part of an even greater campaign unfolding on a higher timeframe.

From this perspective, price charts across different timeframes do not exist independently. They intertwine, influence, and build upon each other. Understanding this connection allows traders to see the market's bigger picture — rather than just isolated skirmishes between Bulls and Bears.

At this point, we have covered the foundation of the Law of Bulls and Bears — from the concept of power and territory, to how each side attacks and defends, and finally to how their battles play out across multiple timeframes. All of this leads to one simple truth: the market is never random; it always moves according to the relative strength between buyers and sellers.

And it is from this law that we can begin to explore deeper — into market structure itself — where every attack, defense, occupation, and counterattack is most clearly reflected on the price chart.

The Formation of Price – Market Structure

Basic Market Structure

After understanding the driving forces and underlying dynamics behind the battle between the Bulls and the Bears, it is time to step back from individual skirmishes and examine the broader market picture. While each attack and defense has its own purpose, it is only when we connect them into a continuous sequence that we begin to see how price forms structure. This framework reflects the entire law of market movement.

Now, let's take a look at the chart in the illustration below.

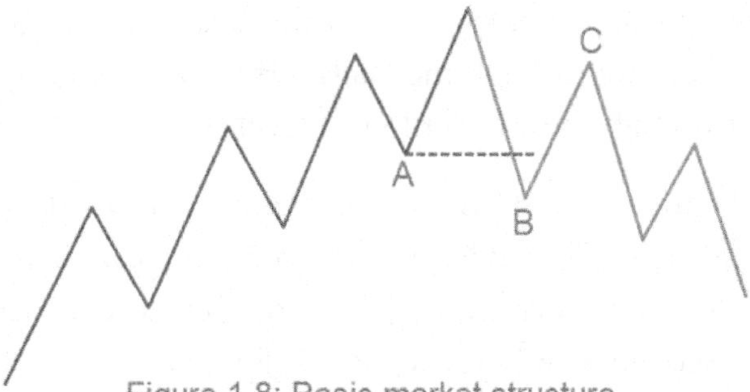

Figure 1.8: Basic market structure

In Figure 1.8, we can see that in an uptrend, the basic market structure is characterized by higher highs and higher lows. This is the stage where the Bulls hold the advantage. The Bulls continue to attack, pushing prices upward, while the Bears attempt to defend by blocking those bullish advances.

On the left side of the figure, the lows represent the Bulls' territories — the areas where price stops falling and begins to rise again. Each time the price touches a low and reverses upward, it marks another failed Bear attack and a successful takeover by the Bulls. Conversely, the highs represent the Bears' territories, where the price turns from rising to falling, showing their efforts to counterattack.

However, in a strong uptrend, the Bulls consistently defend their territories at higher levels than before. This creates a sequence of higher lows — a clear sign of growing buying strength. At the same time, the Bulls continuously attack the Bears' territories, pushing back selling pressure and expanding their control. When a previous high is broken, that zone temporarily shifts from being a Bear territory to becoming a Bull territory, reflecting the Bulls' clear dominance in the market.

At a certain point, as buying momentum begins to weaken, the Bulls can no longer sustain their offensive power. After one final breakout that forms a higher high, the price starts to fall and breaks below the previous low, represented by level A in the illustration. Area A is the Bulls' highest defensive territory, the place where they once protected the uptrend. When this territory is breached, it signals that the Bears have begun to gain the upper hand, breaking through the Bulls' first line of defense and pushing price lower, forming a new lower low at level B.

From here, the market tends to transition from an uptrend to a downtrend. After forming a lower low, the price retraces and creates a new lower high at level C, below the previous peak. Step by step, a new market structure emerges — a sequence of lower highs and lower lows.

However, it is essential to note that the market rarely moves in this textbook-perfect fashion. In most real-world situations, price action is far more complex, filled with hesitation, traps, and unpredictable reversals. These irregular movements often lead traders to misread market structure and enter trades at poor locations. That is why, in the next section, we will analyze a special scenario that frequently deceives traders — to understand how the market truly operates beneath the familiar yet deceptive surface of its price waves.

Advanced Market Structure

Next, we will proceed to the section on advanced market structures. While the basic structure helps us understand the overall framework of how the market operates — where price moves through highs and lows in a relatively orderly pattern — at the advanced level, we will dive deeper into more complex situations, where the underlying structure is revealed through smaller, more intricate price formations.

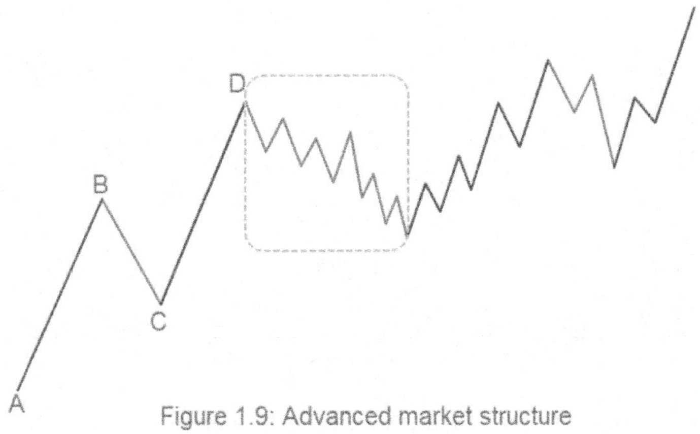

Figure 1.9: Advanced market structure

In Figure 1.9, from point A to point D, we can observe a basic market structure characterized by higher lows and higher highs. At this stage, price continues to break through previous highs, clearly showing an upward trend — consistent with the basic structure we discussed earlier.

However, as the market transitions into the next phase, the movement becomes increasingly complex. From the high at D, the price begins to form smaller downward swings, creating a sequence of lower highs and lower lows. This is the point where many traders make a common mistake:

they see this smaller structure and quickly assume the market has reversed into a downtrend, prompting them to look for short entries.

In reality, these small bearish structures often represent only temporary corrections within a larger bullish trend. The price may fluctuate within a narrow range, giving the illusion of a trend reversal, but in essence, it still moves within the dominant upward structure.

In other words, these smaller structures are simply internal movements within the broader framework. The overall trend truly changes only when the price breaks the major high or low that defines the larger structure. Until that happens, these smaller fluctuations are nothing more than corrections within the ongoing trend — not genuine reversal signals.

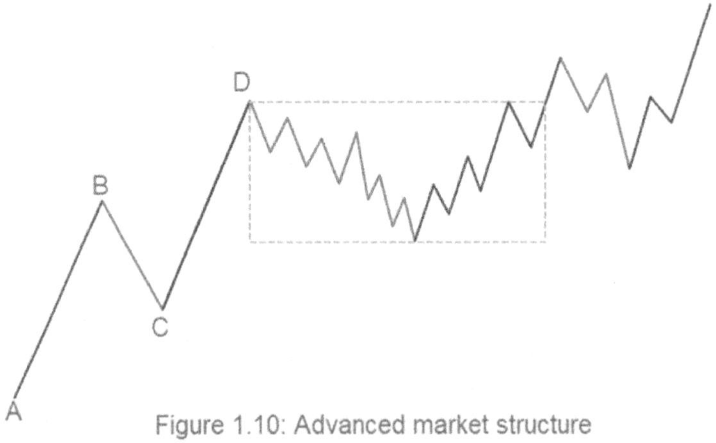

Figure 1.10: Advanced market structure

In the price range highlighted in Figure 1.10, we can see that price can move through various structural patterns — sometimes rising, sometimes falling — yet all of it still occurs within the boundaries of the larger trend (C–D). It is only when price breaks the key high of the major structure (D) that the market truly confirms the continuation of the uptrend.

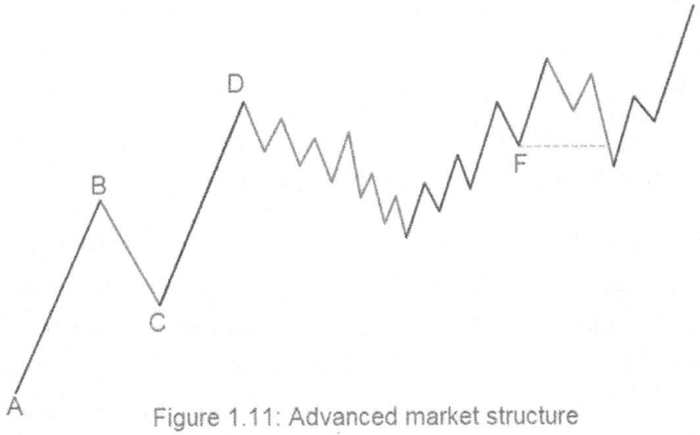

Figure 1.11: Advanced market structure

Another common mistake traders often make occurs right after the price breaks through a key high. When they see the price move above the previous high, they assume the uptrend has been confirmed. As a result, they quickly identify the most recent low as the new major low — in this example, point F. Based on that assumption, if the price later breaks below area F, they believe the bullish structure has been invalidated and that the market is shifting into a downtrend. However, in reality, that is not the case.

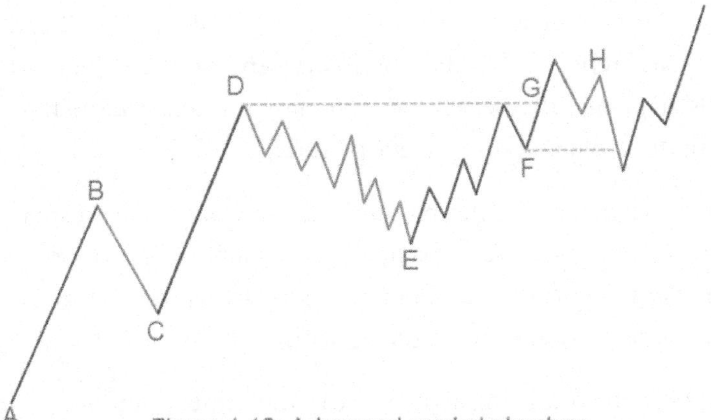

Figure 1.12: Advanced market structure

The true major low of a larger structure must be identified based on the entire context of price movement, not just on small, localized swings. In this example, the lowest point of the whole move from D to G is actually E, not F. In other words, area E represents the Bulls' strong defensive territory, and only when price breaks below this area can we say that the overall bullish structure has truly been violated.

The confusion between a minor low (F) and the major low (E) is what causes many traders to make a series of consecutive mistakes. For instance, after mistakenly identifying F as the key low, they might wait for the price to pull back to F to place a buy order. But when price breaks below F, they assume the trend has reversed and quickly shift to looking for short entries near the next highs, such as area H. As a result, they get caught in a chain of errors — buying at the wrong place, selling at the wrong time — and end up with losses.

In reality, traders who make this mistake are not necessarily wrong; they are simply seeing the market correctly, but within too narrow a picture — missing the control exerted by the larger one.

In the Law of Bulls and Bears, I describe this concept with an easy-to-remember image: the "mother Bull" and "mother Bear," along with their "calves." Traders often focus too much on the actions of the "Bull calves" or "Bear calves" — the smaller movements on lower timeframes — and forget that the market is still under the control of the "mother Bull" or "mother Bear," representing the dominant trend on the higher timeframe. When this happens, they easily get caught up in short-term fluctuations and lose sight of the market's bigger picture.

In reality, within every smaller picture, there are always even smaller ones — and the larger picture we see is itself part of an even greater one beyond it. The market is a continuous chain of nested structures — smaller within larger, and larger within even larger — with no clear boundary.

Typically, I use the following sequence of timeframes: 1 minute, 5 minutes, 15 minutes, 1 hour, 4 hours, daily, weekly, and monthly. For example, suppose you are trading on the 1-hour chart. In that case, the 4-hour timeframe acts as the parent timeframe — showing the broader view — while the 15-minute timeframe serves as the child, allowing you to observe the fine details of price action within each movement on the 1-hour chart.

At this point, we have covered two key components: basic market structure and advanced market structure. The basic structure helps us understand the foundational framework of price movement, where each high and low reflects the ongoing battle between buyers and sellers. The advanced structure expands that view, helping us see that the real market is far more complex, with multiple overlapping structures across different timeframes.

In the next section, we will learn how to identify Bull zones and Bear zones.

How to Identify Bull Zones and Bear Zones

After understanding what Bull zones and Bear zones are, as well as their roles in reflecting buying and selling power in the market, it is now time to move on to the next important part — how to identify these zones on the chart correctly. In this section, we will explore the three most common and effective methods for drawing Bull zones and Bear zones, each derived from the core logic of the Law of Bulls and Bears.

Bull and Bear Zones as Low and High Zones

First, let's look at Bull and Bear zones that form around the highs and lows on the chart. The first step in identifying them is to locate the clear highs or lows on the chart. These are the areas that reflect a shift in control between buyers and sellers.

We start by identifying the highest or lowest point within each zone. These points serve as the starting markers for the Bull zone or Bear zone, from which we can then draw the zones according to the following principles:

- For zones with long wicks, draw a rectangle that covers the entire wick area.
- For zones with short wicks, draw from the highest or lowest point of that area to the end of the candle body.
- When multiple highs or lows are located close to each other, combine them into a single unified zone.
- If the wick is very long but the candle body is short, include the candle body within the zone to maintain a more balanced and visually clear drawing.

Figure 1.13: Bull/Bear Zones

Of course, we should not draw every Bull or Bear zone based on every high or low on the chart. We should only draw the Bull and Bear zones that are clearly visible, exhibit strong price reactions, and are easily recognizable. If we mark too many zones, the chart will become messy and lose its focus, making the analysis more difficult.

Bull and Bear Zones as Broken Highs and Lows

Figure 1.14: Bull/Bear Zones

In actual trading, broken highs or lows can also serve as potential Bull or Bear zones. However, when applying this to the chart, we do not necessarily need to draw all of these zones, because marking every single one would make the chart cluttered and difficult to read. Instead, it is better to keep these broken highs and lows in mind visually and observe how the price reacts when it returns to retest those areas.

Bull and Bear Zones as the Start of Strong Price Momentum

Figure 1.15: Bull/Bear Zones

Another type of Bull or Bear zone that traders should pay close attention to is the area where strong impulses begin — also known as momentum zones. These are areas where price breaks out with significant strength, indicating clear intervention from one side, even when there may not be a distinct high or low in that region.

For example, in Figure 1.15, we can see a price area that does not form a clear high or low, yet from that point, a sharp upward move begins. This sudden acceleration reflects the Bulls' strong offensive power; therefore, the starting area can be identified as a Bull zone. Likewise, when a strong downward move originates from a particular area, that area is considered a Bear zone.

Some zones will show clear highs or lows. However, many will not — and in those cases, the strength of the momentum itself becomes the key indicator for identifying important price barriers.

At this point, we have covered the three main methods for identifying Bull and Bear zones: locating clear highs and lows, recognizing zones that have been broken, and observing the starting points of strong price momentum. Bull and Bear zones not only help us understand which side is currently in control of the market, but more importantly, they form the foundation for identifying areas to buy and sell in trading.

Buy Zones and Sell Zones

In this section, we will explore another important concept: Buy Zones and Sell Zones, and how they differ from the Bull and Bear zones we studied earlier.

In fact, Buy and Sell zones are specific types of Bull and Bear zones. The key difference lies in their purpose of use. While Bull and Bear zones help us identify areas where buyers or sellers previously held control of the market, Buy and Sell zones represent the areas where we actively look for trading opportunities — in other words, where we plan to buy or sell.

Put simply, Buy and Sell zones are refined and conditional versions of Bull and Bear zones.

For a zone to be considered a valid Buy or Sell zone, it must meet additional confirmation criteria. Therefore, it is essential to recognize that every Buy or Sell zone is either a Bull or Bear zone, but not every Bull or Bear zone qualifies as a Buy or Sell zone.

A Buy zone can be understood as an area where multiple factors align to support a potential upward move. If we view each price zone on the chart as a neutral point with roughly a 50% chance of reversal, then each additional factor that supports the bullish scenario increases our probability of success.

For example:

- If the higher timeframe market structure supports an upward trend, we can increase the probability **by about 5%.**

- Conversely, if the zone is weak, price reactions are unclear, or a nearby Bear zone is creating resistance, we can subtract a portion of that probability accordingly.

Similarly, a Sell zone can be understood as an area where multiple factors align to support the likelihood of a downward move. Suppose we treat each price zone as a neutral point with roughly a 50% chance of reversal. In that case, each factor that strengthens the bearish scenario — such as a higher timeframe downtrend, strong selling pressure from a previous zone, or a clear reversal signal — increases the probability of success for a sell trade.

Figure 1.16: Buy/Sell Zones

Let's take a look at a specific example on the chart. Here, we can identify a Bear zone above and a Bull zone below. However, upon closer observation, we can see that the current market structure is clearly in an uptrend, with buying power dominating and bullish momentum much stronger than selling pressure. Therefore, the Bull zone below — where buyers are likely to step in and push the price upward — receives stronger supporting factors.

Conversely, the Bear zone above contradicts the prevailing uptrend, indicating that seeking sell opportunities there entails a higher level of risk.

In this context, we would not label the Bear zone as a Sell zone. Instead, the Bull zone below would be considered a Buy zone, because it aligns with the existing market structure and offers a higher probability of success.

Reading Market Structure

We have now covered all the essential foundations of the Law of Bulls and Bears — from understanding the balance of power between the two sides, to how price structures are formed, and how to identify Bull and Bear zones as well as Buy and Sell zones. Now it is time to put all those pieces together to see the complete picture of the market.

In the final section of this chapter, we will examine several market structures to understand what they truly reveal. This is the key transition point — moving from understanding the theory of market structure to actually reading real structures on the chart.

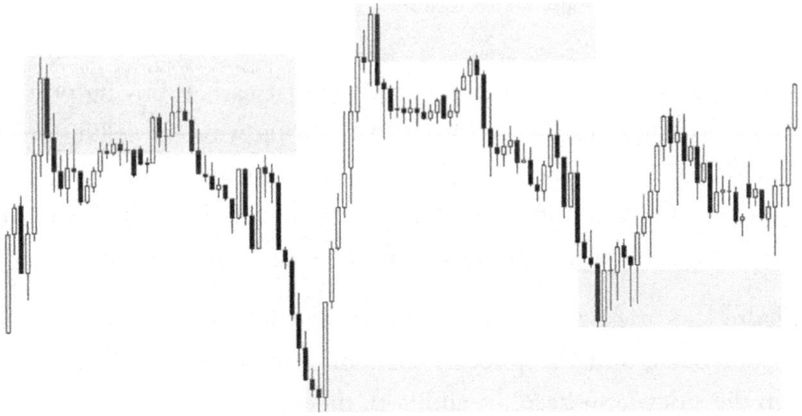

Figure 1.17: Bull-Bear Market Structure

Figure 1.17 presents a sideways price range. The first step is to mark the nearest Bull and Bear zones relative to the current price. However, during this ranging phase, it is important to determine whether buying power or selling power is currently being prioritized.

Figure 1.18: Bull-Bear Market Structure

When we zoom out the chart, we can see that earlier, buying power had strengthened significantly, followed by a strong wave of selling pressure. As the price reached the Bull zone, the Bulls pushed it upward; when it approached the Bear zone, the Bears drove it back down. This tug-of-war between the two sides continues up to the current price level.

In Figure 1.18, the Bears' momentum is being held back by a strong barrier from the Bulls, and the price is forming higher lows and higher highs within the sideways phase. In addition, the slope of the waves created by the Bears is gradually flattening, and the length of those waves is becoming shorter. This shows that the Bears' offensive power is weakening. In this case, we would give more weight to the buy-side scenario. What we should wait for now is clear offensive action from the Bulls — strong bullish candles with visible momentum that can drive price out of the sideways range.

It is important to note that even when we lean toward the buy scenario, we should not enter a trade until additional supporting factors appear — such as a clear entry signal or a favorable risk-to-reward ratio (R:R). If those conditions are not met, it is better to stay out. All of these supporting factors for trade entries will be revealed in the following chapters of this book.

Let's move on to the next example.

Figure 1.19: Bull-Bear Market Structure

In Figure 1.19, we draw the nearest Bull and Bear zones relative to the current price. On the right side of the chart, the market exhibits a bearish structure, characterized by lower highs and lower lows. However, the prior bullish momentum was quite strong, with several Bull zones established across the left half of the chart.

We can see that, in the short term, the Bears are currently in control; however, in the longer term, the Bulls still hold greater strength. Although the structure is not entirely sideways, both sides have supporting factors. The Bull and Bear zones are relatively close to each other, which makes entering trades in this kind of market highly risky.

In this situation, if we plan to buy, we should wait for the price to break above the Bear zone and form a bullish structure. Conversely, if we are looking to sell, we should wait for clear bearish candles showing strong dominance from the Bears, while also assessing whether the R:R ratio is favorable.

This is a case where neither side holds full control — a challenging situation that traders often face. In contrast, when the trend is clear, such as during a strong bullish phase where the Bears' resistance appears weak, the logical approach would be to look for buy opportunities.

By now, you've made it through the first stretch of this journey — the part where we begin to truly understand how the market works beneath the surface. From the very first principles of the Law of Bulls and Bears, you've seen that behind every price movement lies a constant tug-of-war between buyers and sellers — a never-ending battle where every candle, every surge, and every pullback carries a story of its own.

From there, we took a deeper dive into market structure — learning to read price through the rhythm of highs and lows, to recognize why there are times when price surges powerfully, drifts sideways, or suddenly collapses without warning. You've also learned to distinguish between Bull and Bear zones versus Buy and Sell zones — how to draw them correctly, and how to use them as your compass when planning trades with an edge.

And finally, through the section on reading market structure, you've started to see the market in a completely new light. What once looked chaotic now feels organized; what once seemed random now reveals intention and order. The price chart is no longer a blur of noise — it's a living battlefield of momentum, logic, and emotion.

Everything we've built so far forms the very first foundation — the solid ground on which you'll stand as we move forward into the next stage of this book: applying what you've learned to identify high-probability entries and build real confidence in your trading.

The market won't get easier from here — but your understanding will. Let's keep going.

CHAPTER 2: INTERNAL ENHANCERS

In this chapter, we will explore the trading strategy that will serve as the foundation throughout this entire book — the Breakout strategy. This is one of the most popular and effective trading methods, built upon a simple principle: trade in the direction where the market is breaking out. However, no breakout setup is flawless on its own. A trade becomes truly robust only when a series of factors support it — each one quietly enhancing its probability of success. That is why I refer to them as **enhancers**.

You can think of each enhancer as an added layer of strength around your setup. They do not make the method more complicated; they simply make it more stable and reliable. From this point forward, our aim is to elevate an ordinary breakout trade into a high-probability one by deliberately incorporating these enhancers, step by step.

This chapter focuses on decoding supportive internal enhancers — the intrinsic factors within the setup itself, without yet considering the broader market context. These internal components form the first layer of evaluation for judging how trustworthy a breakout pattern truly is.

Once you learn to recognize and combine these internal enhancers, you'll stop seeing breakouts as random events. Instead, you'll start viewing them as structured, logical patterns — setups with measurable probabilities of success. From there, you'll move one step closer to building a breakout trading system that operates with both stability and consistency in real market conditions.

Applied Strategy: Breakout Trading

The Breakout strategy is more than just a trading method — it is the bridge that connects price action, market structure, and the never-ending battle between Bulls and Bears. Every time price breaks out of a key zone — whether it's a high or a low — one side is fighting to seize control from the other. And it's precisely in those moments that all the concepts we studied in Chapter 1 — market structure, Bull and Bear zones, Buy and Sell zones — come together and show their full power. A breakout doesn't exist in isolation; it is the direct result of a shift in balance between supply and demand, pressure and release, defense and offense between the two sides.

What makes this strategy particularly effective is that it aligns perfectly with the natural rhythm of the market: movement through trends. When price breaks a key structure or a major zone, it's not just a technical signal — it's the market revealing its chosen direction. In other words, a strong breakout is the clearest expression of the timeless principle *"trend is friend"* — the trend is the trader's most reliable ally. Instead of trying to predict reversals, traders who follow breakouts choose to move with the side that's winning.

Moreover, a breakout is the purest reflection of price action itself. Every candle formed during consolidation, every test of a zone, and every burst of price momentum mirrors market psychology — the hopes, fears, and reactions of the crowd, captured in movement. When you learn to read breakouts, you are actually learning to read human emotion and collective behavior, distilled into price. That's why breakout trading represents price action at its most refined and logical form — no need for complex indicators, only a deep understanding of how price moves and reacts.

This strategy works equally well for both new and experienced traders. For beginners, breakout trading offers a clear and structured framework — it helps them understand *why* prices move and *when* to take action. For experienced traders, it provides a deeper layer of insight — beyond simply "breaks or not," it becomes about reading structure, recognizing power dynamics, and combining multiple factors to isolate the highest-probability setups.

Ultimately, breakout trading is not just a strategy — it is the common language of the market, a way to read and trade that every serious trader must learn to speak fluently.

Before diving into the technical elements within the setup, let's revisit the core concept of the Breakout trading strategy. The term *breakout* literally means "to break through" — and in the context of trading, it describes the moment when price pushes beyond a key barrier, signaling that one side has gained dominance over the other.

In other words, breakout trading means entering the market at the point where the price bursts out of a range or structure that had previously contained it. It is the moment when balance gives way to momentum — when the market reveals which side, Bull or Bear, is taking control.

Let's look at the following illustration, set within the context of a bullish market structure.

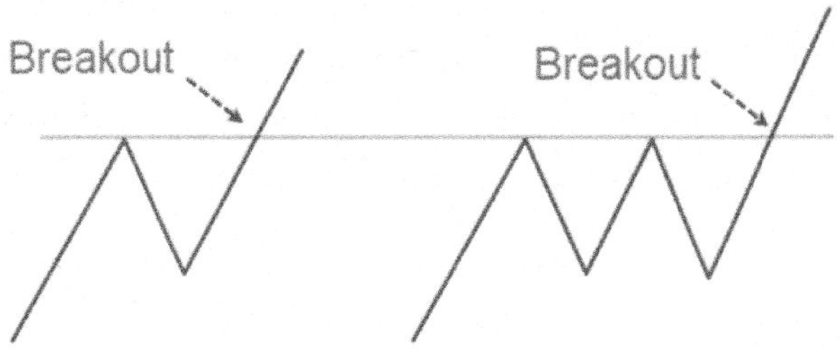

Figure 2.1: Breakout Pattern

From the perspective of the Bulls and Bears theory, when the market forms a high or a zone of highs, that area represents where the Bears currently hold the upper hand — clearly shown by price being pushed down from that region. The high zone, therefore, serves as the Bears' defensive territory, the area they strive to protect to prevent the Bulls from advancing.

When price breaks above this high, it signifies that the Bears have failed in their attempt to defend their ground, and the Bulls have taken control. The strength of the buying force at this moment is powerful enough to push the price beyond the zone that the Bears previously dominated.

That is why, in breakout trading, the first and most crucial condition is that the price must clearly break through a defined barrier. As shown in the illustration, when the price breaks above a high, it indicates that the Bulls have gained dominance, and we prioritize looking for buying opportunities.

However, real trading is never that simple. Seeing a price break through a resistance zone doesn't mean we should enter a trade immediately. The breakout itself is only the first condition — the "open gate," signaling the potential beginning of a new trend. For a breakout setup to truly have a high probability of success, we need to evaluate additional technical elements — the confirming signs, also known as the *supportive internal enhancers.*

In the following sections, we will examine these enhancers individually. You will see that behind every clean breakout lies a subtle yet intense battle between Bulls and Bears — where market logic, crowd psychology, and price action converge to form a complete scenario for the next trading opportunity.

Internal Enhancer 1 – Equal Highs or Lows

In this section, we will take the first step toward building high-quality breakout entries, using the context of an uptrend. A good entry point doesn't come from luck — it begins with the ability to correctly read the balance between the two sides of the market, especially the moment when the Bears start to lose strength and the Bulls begin to take control.

In practice, the more dominant the Bulls become, the stronger the upward momentum tends to be, and the higher the probability that the uptrend will continue. Therefore, our task is to identify areas where selling pressure has weakened — where the Bears no longer have enough power to push price lower, and the Bulls are preparing to regain control.

To better understand this mechanism, let's examine two classic scenarios below — where we can clearly observe how the Bears gradually lose momentum and how the Bulls reclaim control of the market.

Scenario 1: Single-High Breakout

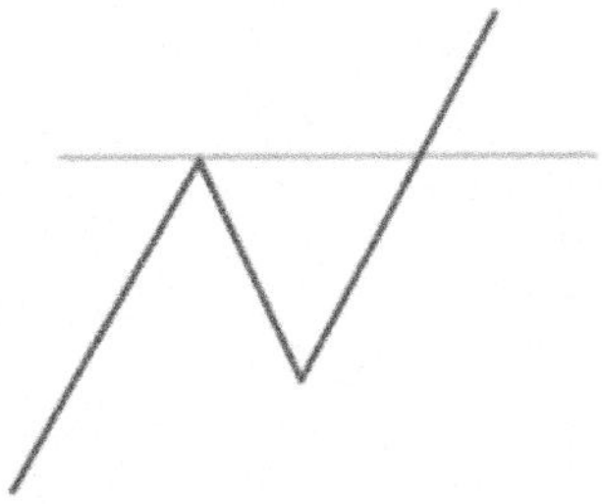

Figure 2.2: Single-High Breakout

Let's imagine a chart where a clear high zone has formed, as illustrated. Before reaching this zone, the Bulls were in control, driving price upward with strong momentum until the market reached the high. However, once the price approached this area, the Bears began to counterattack, pushing the price back down. This high zone, therefore, becomes an area of concentrated supply — a region where a large number of sell orders are triggered, including positions from institutions and large funds.

When the price is pushed down, not all sell orders at the high are executed. A significant portion remains "pending" in that area, waiting to be filled once the price returns. Consequently, when the price rises again and approaches the high, those remaining sell orders begin to get filled gradually. If the remaining sell volume is fully absorbed while the buying pressure remains strong, the price will continue to rise, breaking above the previous high.

That moment marks the point where the Bulls officially regain control, and the broken high becomes a clear breakout signal.

Scenario 2: Multi-High Breakout

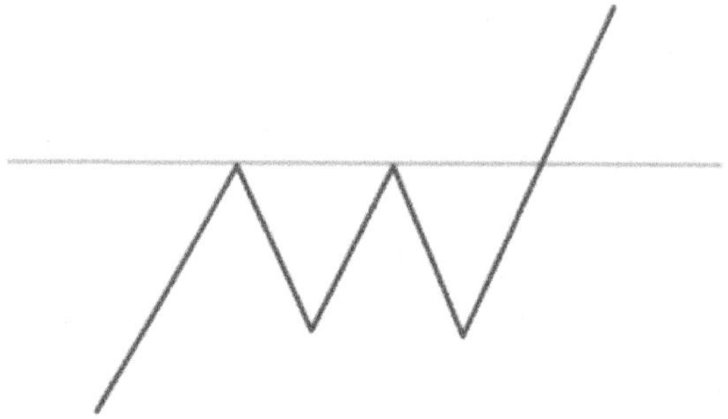

Figure 2.3: Multi-High Breakout

In this same example, if the buying pressure is fully absorbed while the selling pressure remains strong, the price will fail to break through the high zone and will instead reverse downward. At that point, the Bears temporarily take control, pushing the price away from the resistance area. For the Bulls to regain control, they must gather stronger forces and launch a new offensive powerful enough to break through at least two highs — in other words, to penetrate the territories still held by the Bears.

From that, we can see two distinct breakout scenarios. In the first, the Bulls only need to break through a single high to trigger a breakout. In the second, the Bulls must break through two or more highs to create a successful breakout.

This leads us to an important question: between these two cases, which scenario provides stronger support for a breakout trade?

As mentioned earlier, when there is only one high, it indicates that the Bears have intervened just once — they successfully managed to push the price down, but their participation remains limited. However, when multiple highs form within the same price area, the meaning changes entirely. It indicates that the Bears have repeatedly entered the market, engaging in several rounds of defense against the Bulls.

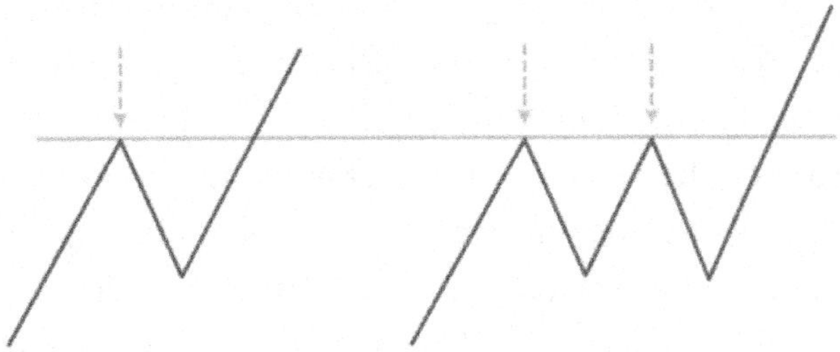

Figure 2.4: Ideal Breakout

From that, we can compare the difference between two situations: price breaking through a single high versus price breaking through a zone with multiple equal highs.

When several highs form within the same price area, it shows that the Bears have made repeated, determined efforts to defend their territory. Each time the price returns to this zone, the Bears strengthen their forces, adding more sell orders in an attempt to maintain their defensive line. Such repeated participation reveals that they are committing their full strength to prevent the Bulls from taking control of that price level.

Therefore, when a zone with multiple equal highs is finally broken, the psychological and technical impact of the breakout is far greater. Once the Bears' defensive line collapses, a wave of stop-loss orders from their side gets triggered simultaneously. This cascade of buy orders, combined with existing bullish pressure, creates a powerful breakout move that pushes the price farther than a breakout through a single high.

Now, let's imagine this from the familiar perspective of the ongoing battle between Bulls and Bears. Suppose I take the role of the Bears, commanding an army of one hundred soldiers. I have two possible ways to respond, each corresponding to one of the two breakout scenarios above.

- **Scenario 1: Tactical Retreat.** When the Bulls attack and push into my price zone, I might send out only ten of my soldiers to push the price back down — just to test how strong the opposing force really is. But soon after, the Bulls strike back with overwhelming momentum, driving the price even higher and reclaiming the territory I had just defended. In a situation like this, I may choose to pull back temporarily, allowing price to move higher toward another area — one where I've already stationed my main forces. There, I can launch a stronger counterattack, pushing the price back down and regaining control of the market. I'm able to do this because I still have ninety soldiers in reserve, ready to fight another round.

- **Scenario 2: Holding the Line.** If I, as the Bears, choose to hold my ground, the situation becomes far more complicated. When the price rises to the resistance zone, I send out ten soldiers to defend it. But the Bulls don't stop there — they continue their assault with even greater strength. To maintain my position, I have no choice but to deploy more troops, wave after wave, doing everything I can to hold the line. Each time price forms another high within the same zone, it reflects the fact that I — the Bears — have had to send out more forces again and again to defend this territory from being taken. But if, after all these efforts, I still fail and price finally breaks through the zone I've been fortifying, it means the Bulls are truly stronger. I've exhausted my entire army, fought to the end, yet still couldn't stop price from moving higher. In that context, the probability of price continuing to surge upward is extremely high — because at that point, I am out of strength, and all the selling pressure within the resistance zone has been almost completely absorbed.

You see, when multiple highs appear on the chart, it's a clear sign that the Bears have attempted to defend their position several times. And when such a strong side still ends up being defeated, it means their opponent — the Bulls — are even stronger by a significant margin. Once you understand this, you'll realize that a breakout through a zone with multiple equal highs often carries far greater momentum, and price tends to travel much farther than in a breakout through a single high.

Based on this understanding, we draw a horizontal line parallel to the time axis, passing through the highs or lows to clearly define the barrier zone — this is what we call the breakout level.

Now, let's look at the first condition required for a high-quality breakout trade: *There must be at least two equal highs or lows at the breakout level.*

When I say "at least two highs or lows," it means that in reality, the scenario may involve price breaking through three, four, or even more highs or lows. The more highs or lows that are taken out, the more it shows that the attacking side has defeated its opponent multiple times — and the greater the likelihood that the price will travel farther after the breakout.

However, to make the concept easier to visualize and help you fully grasp the underlying principle, I will use the double high/double low structure as the standard model for all subsequent analyses throughout this book.

Once the breakout level has been clearly identified, we can apply the basic entry principle shown below. This serves as the foundation for you to become familiar with the pattern. As we progress through the following sections, we will gradually refine and expand this set of trading rules into a complete, high-probability breakout system.

Basic Break Entry

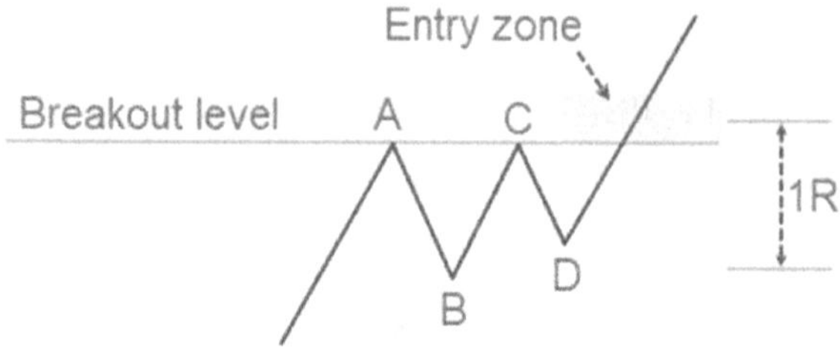

Figure 2.5: Basic break entry

The basic break entry is illustrated in Figure 2.5, which shows a bullish breakout setup. In this example, the two highs are labeled A and C. The low formed after high A is marked as point B, while the low formed after high C is point D. When the price breaks above the resistance zone — the breakout level — that moment marks the confirmation of the breakout pattern.

The key to this principle lies precisely at the moment when the price breaks through the breakout level. That breakout represents the Bears' weakening momentum and the Bulls' takeover of control, as they successfully push the price beyond a resistance area that had previously stopped the market multiple times. This signals that the bullish trend is being reinforced, and the probability of the price continuing higher is significantly increased.

The basic break entry is defined as follows:

- Price closes above the breakout level.
- The closer the entry is to the breakout level, the better.
- Stop-loss is placed below point D.

The stop-loss is placed just below point D because this area represents the Bull territory — the defensive zone of the buyers. The role of this Bull zone is to hold the price when the market makes a minor pullback or correction after the breakout. If price returns and breaks below this level, it means the Bulls have failed to defend their territory, and the buy position should be exited. Therefore, the area below point D is the most logical place to set the stop-loss.

The distance from the entry point (near the breakout level) to the stop-loss (below point D) is called 1R — the basic risk unit of the trade. Based on this, profit targets can be set in multiples of R — for example, 2R, 3R, or higher — depending on the strength of the ongoing trend.

The purpose of introducing the basic break entry is not to present a final, perfected entry method. Instead, it serves as a foundational model—something simple and clear—for us to visualize how an entry works as we start optimizing in this chapter. By beginning with a basic framework, it becomes much easier to see how each enhancer strengthens the setup and improves our timing. In Chapter 4, after all key elements have been refined, I will present the fully optimized entry model that you can apply with confidence.

Notes:

One important point to keep in mind is that the breakout level should not be defined as a wide price zone. If you draw it as an area, it becomes difficult to pinpoint the exact level where the price truly breaks out, which creates ambiguity when deciding on an entry. Instead, the breakout level should be represented as a clear horizontal line — a precise boundary between the Bulls and the Bears. Once the price closes decisively beyond that line, the breakout can be confirmed with confidence.

In cases where the two highs are not perfectly aligned — for example, when one high is significantly higher or lower than the other — the pattern loses its balance. This reflects uneven buying strength at different price levels and indicates that the Bulls' momentum is not evenly distributed. Such inconsistency weakens the overall setup and lowers the probability of a successful breakout. Based on real market statistics, the more horizontally aligned the highs are, the greater the chance that the price will continue in the breakout direction afterward. Conversely, the more uneven the highs, the less reliable the setup becomes.

That said, nothing in trading is absolute. Minor discrepancies — such as a slight difference between the two highs — can still be acceptable, especially when other factors, like market structure, key zones, or strong momentum candles, support the setup.

In later chapters, you'll learn how to analyze market statistics and backtest these variations to clearly see the difference between clean, well-aligned setups and those with slight imbalances. This practice not only strengthens your understanding of trading probabilities but also sharpens your ability to assess the "quality" of a breakout setup based on real market data — an essential skill for identifying high-probability breakout entries.

Figure 2.6: Breakout example

Figure 2.6 provides an example that meets the criteria of having two relatively equal lows in a bearish breakout setup. If you look closely, you'll notice that the second low is slightly lower than the first one; however, the difference is minimal. Moreover, the small variation occurs only in the candle wick, which means we can confidently take the trade without worrying too much about this minor discrepancy.

In this same example, placing the stop-loss just above the second high of the pattern (point D) is a sufficiently safe approach. Although price retraces upward briefly, it does not reach the stop-loss level. After that, the price resumes its downward movement, continuing the momentum of the breakout.

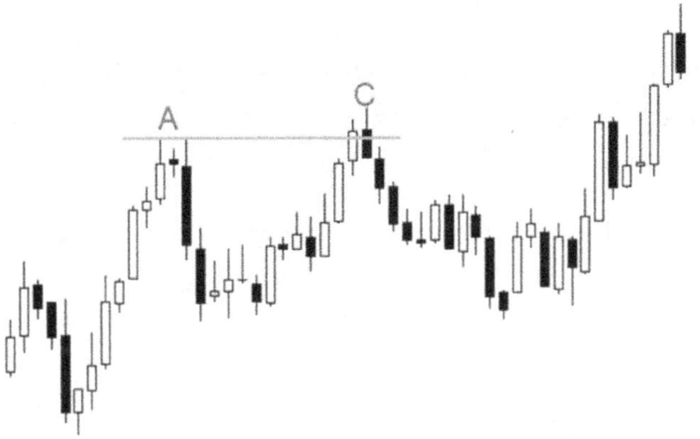

Figure 2.7: Breakout example

In Figure 2.7, we once again see a bullish breakout pattern. This time, High C is slightly higher than High A. However, unlike the previous example, this setup would not be considered valid. The reason is that High C closes above High A, indicating that the two sides — the Bulls and the Bears — are not engaging evenly at the same price levels. This imbalance shows that buying and selling pressure is unevenly distributed. As a result, the breakout level can no longer be seen as a reliable boundary, which reduces the overall quality and effectiveness of the breakout setup.

This brings us to the first internal enhancer for breakout trading: the more equal the two highs or two lows are at the breakout level, the stronger and more reliable the setup becomes. However, this is only one piece of the larger puzzle. A truly high-quality entry does not depend on a single factor — it is the result of multiple conditions aligning together.

Internal Enhancer 2 – Price Range

The second internal enhancer we'll explore is **price range** — in other words, the way price waves move within the breakout pattern. This factor vividly reflects the "breathing rhythm" of the market before a true breakout occurs. By observing how the price range evolves, we can gauge not only the degree of market accumulation but also the potential strength and distance of the upcoming breakout move.

In this section, we'll analyze how these price swings behave within a breakout setup, why a narrowing range is a positive sign, and what kind of contraction is considered ideal for a strong breakout.

Let's take a look at the wave structure in Figure 2.8. Here, we once again have four key points — A, B, C, and D — forming the price movement before the breakout unfolds.

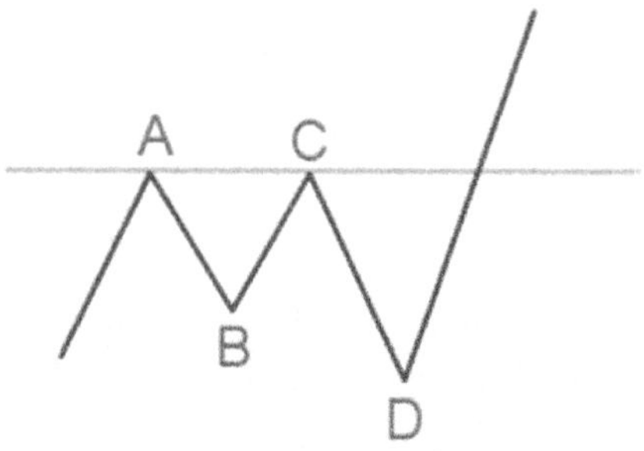

Figure 2.8: Breakout pattern analysis

In a bullish breakout setup, if D is positioned lower than B, the market falls into an unfavorable situation. In this case, price has swept both the previous low (B) and the previous highs (A–C). In other words, the market has "cleared both sides" — shaking out both buyers and sellers — which makes the structure unstable and prone to entering a choppy, directionless consolidation phase.

Furthermore, when D lies below B, another consequence arises: the stop-loss zone becomes significantly wider. This means that, to achieve a favorable R:R ratio, the price would have to travel farther after the breakout. In reality, such setups tend to be less effective, as the large price range makes risk control more difficult.

From these observations, we can draw an important structural rule for breakout setups: D should not be lower than B.

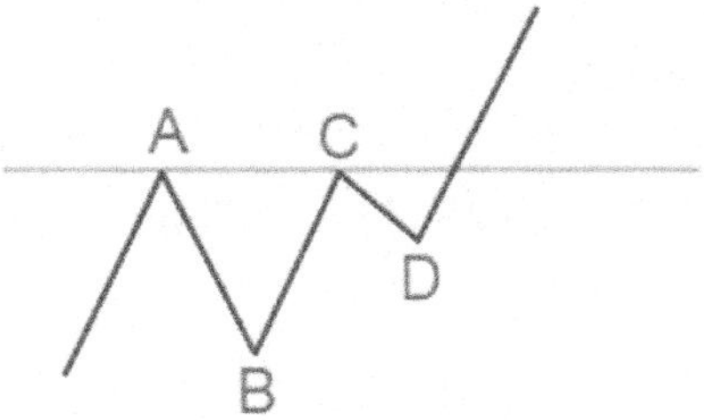

Figure 2.9: Breakout pattern analysis

Now let's look at the opposite scenario — when D is positioned much higher than B (Figure 2.9). In this case, the structure of the pattern also becomes unbalanced. Specifically, from High A, the Bears initially show strong selling pressure, but by the time the price reaches High C, that pressure has weakened noticeably, making the retracement from C to D too shallow. This large disparity reflects an unstable market condition, where the balance of power between the two sides shifts abruptly, causing the overall price movement to lose its natural rhythm.

In addition, if D forms too narrowly — with small, unclear candles or almost no meaningful pullback — another issue arises: the stop-loss is no longer safe. When price creates only a short, shallow retracement before the breakout, the stop-loss often sits too close to the entry, making the position more vulnerable to being hit.

Therefore, to form a well-balanced breakout pattern with healthy price waves, D should ideally lie within the lower half of the A–B swing. When this condition is met, the range of the pattern is wide enough to reflect proper accumulation and a clear test of supply and demand, while also ensuring that the stop-loss is placed at a reasonable, safer distance.

At this point, we have the second internal enhancer for breakout trading:

- D should be located within the lower half of the A–B swing.

When measuring this, we take the lowest point of the move — including the candle wick. This approach ensures that the pattern's range accurately reflects the true market condition while helping the breakout setup maintain a safer stop-loss placement and a higher probability of success.

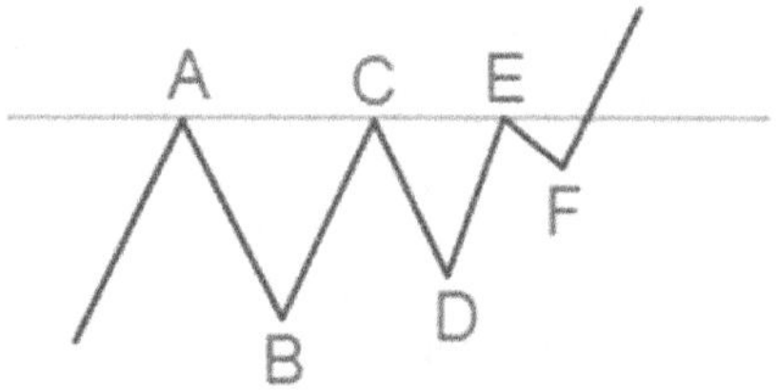

Figure 2.10: Breakout pattern analysis

There are times when the pattern may present a special situation, as shown in Figure 2.10. We still have all the key structural points — A, B, C, and D — but afterward, price may react strongly at a new area, forming another low, which we'll temporarily label as F. This low at F lies noticeably higher than D, yet this does not invalidate the pattern because the main structure remains intact. In this case, the setup is still considered valid, and according to the basic rule, the standard stop-loss should still be placed below D.

However, there are situations where price shows a strong reaction at point F — for example, a large bullish engulfing candle or a clear cluster of candles demonstrating solid buying momentum. When that happens, we can consider moving the stop-loss higher — specifically, placing it below

F. This stop-loss adjustment is a flexible approach that allows you to reduce risk and improve the reward-to-risk ratio, but it should only be applied when there is clear evidence of strong momentum in that area.

The key here is that such adjustments must be verified through market statistics and backtesting. If, after multiple samples, placing the stop-loss at F consistently produces a satisfactory win rate, then this modification can be incorporated into your strategy. On the other hand, if the reaction zone at F is frequently breached, keeping the stop-loss at D will remain the safer and more reliable choice.

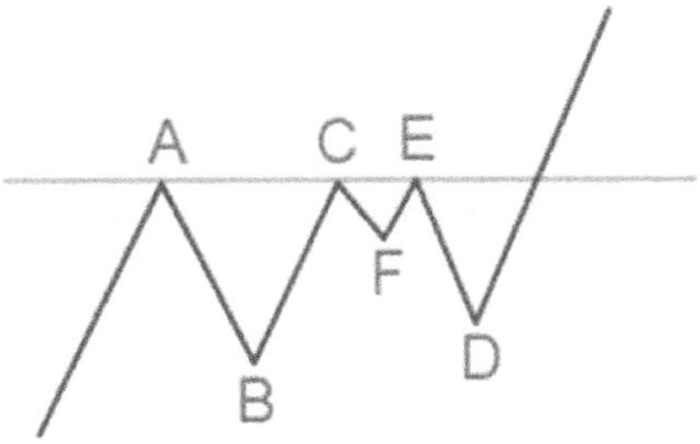

Figure 2.11: Breakout pattern analysis

Next, let's examine another scenario that frequently arises in real market conditions. After forming point C, the price may continue to create an additional point E. At first glance, the pattern still seems to meet the basic structural requirements of a breakout setup. However, there's a subtle detail that affects its quality: the pattern shows a small "protrusion" at the low, forming point F.

When we analyze the balance of power between the two sides in this situation, the picture becomes clear. Initially, the Bears push strongly downward to create low B. Price then retraces upward toward resistance, but the selling pressure weakens — as shown by the relatively shallow pullback to F. However, the Bulls then fail to break above the previous high, and the Bears regain strength, driving the price down again to form low D.

In cases like this, the setup should not be discarded completely, but it requires extra caution. When the range of the pattern becomes distorted, it indicates that the probability of success has decreased. To compensate for that increased risk, you need additional confirming factors — for example, a strong higher-timeframe trend or clear bullish momentum supporting the breakout direction.

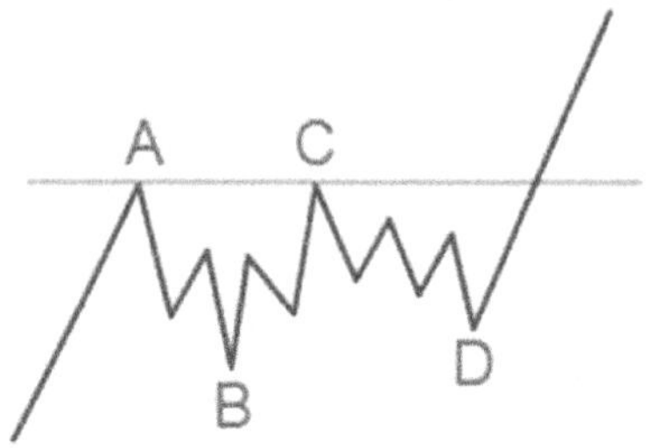

Figure 2.12: Breakout pattern analysis

Another situation that makes the pattern's range less ideal is when price forms the structure *within* the active swing itself. In other words, instead of creating clean and balanced waves from one point to another, the market continuously forms small highs and lows inside the main movement. This behavior indicates that the Bulls and Bears are still fiercely battling at lower levels, which disrupts the price flow and causes the overall market rhythm to lose coherence.

In contrast, a breakout pattern is considered clean and well-formed when each segment of movement — for example, from A to B, from B to C, or from C to D — develops as a single, clear wave without excessive fluctuations within it. When price swings move in this smooth and uninterrupted manner, the structure becomes harmonious. These are the kinds of patterns, with well-defined range and clean wave movement, that tend to produce stronger and more stable breakouts.

Below are some examples of patterns with poor range quality.

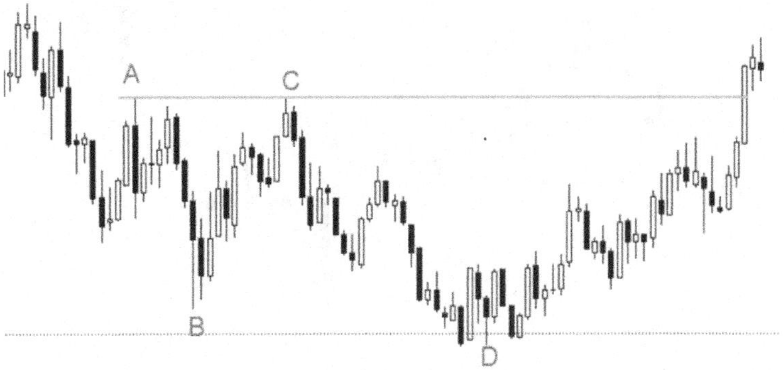

Figure 2.13: Breakout example

In Figure 2.13, although the pattern satisfies the first internal enhancer (with A and C positioned at roughly the same level), the overall range of the pattern is not ideal. First, D is lower than B. In addition, from point C, the price structure unfolds through several small swings before forming low D. While the C–D movement still reflects selling dominance, the battle between the Bulls and Bears during this phase is uneven. Therefore, this setup is not an ideal breakout pattern to trade.

Figure 2.14: Breakout example

Figure 2.14 shows a well-structured bullish breakout pattern — a setup that is quite ideal for trading. Two equal highs form the breakout level, the price range is balanced, and D lies within the lower half of the A–B swing. The waves within the pattern are also clean and distinct, without excessive fluctuations or false highs and lows that could distort the structure.

With this, we conclude the second internal enhancer — price range. The range within a breakout pattern is not just about the distance between points; it reflects how the market expresses its rhythm. A pattern with a harmonious range and clear, uninterrupted swings shows that the forces between the two sides are being properly absorbed and balanced — a sign that the market is compressing energy for a genuine breakout. In contrast, when the range becomes distorted, waves appear choppy, or the structure looks chaotic, it reveals instability and reduces the overall reliability of the setup.

Internal Enhancer 3 – Break Candle

The third internal enhancer in a breakout pattern is the *break candle* — the candle that actually breaks through a resistance or support level, marking the precise moment when the breakout pattern becomes active. This is the most crucial point in the entire setup, as it reveals the outcome of the battle between the two sides — which one is stronger, and which one truly holds control over the market.

In this section, we'll take a closer look at what defines a strong break candle and how to interpret the message behind its structure to determine whether a breakout is truly reliable. This is the key to distinguishing a genuine market expansion from a mere test of strength before a potential reversal.

Figure 2.15: Breakout candle

Let's consider two breakout patterns shown in Figure 2.15, where the price breaks upward. According to the rules of a valid breakout, the break candle must close *above* the breakout level to be considered a confirmed signal. This is the most basic condition for distinguishing a genuine breakout from a temporary market test.

However, not every candle that closes above the breakout level carries a positive meaning. In the pattern on the left side of the figure, if the candle has a long upper wick, it indicates that while the Bulls tried to push the price higher, the Bears launched a strong counterattack, pulling the price back down significantly before the candle closed. As a result, even though the candle closes above the breakout level, the long wick reveals that selling pressure is still present — the Bulls haven't fully taken control yet.

In the pattern on the right, the candle merely *wicked through* the breakout level before collapsing and closing back below it. In many cases, the price may later break through the level again with a subsequent candle, but by that time, the breakout level has already been "contaminated" — the Bears still have a presence there. Therefore, even if a breakout eventually occurs, the untested Bear zone left behind by the earlier long-wick candle still poses a high risk of the price being pushed back down.

From these examples, we can draw an important conclusion: break candles with long wicks are typically *bad signals*. They reveal indecision or a lack of commitment in buying strength — and sometimes, they're even signs of stop-hunting moves engineered by large players to shake out retail traders. When you encounter such setups, it's best to stay cautious — the market may not yet be ready for a genuine breakout.

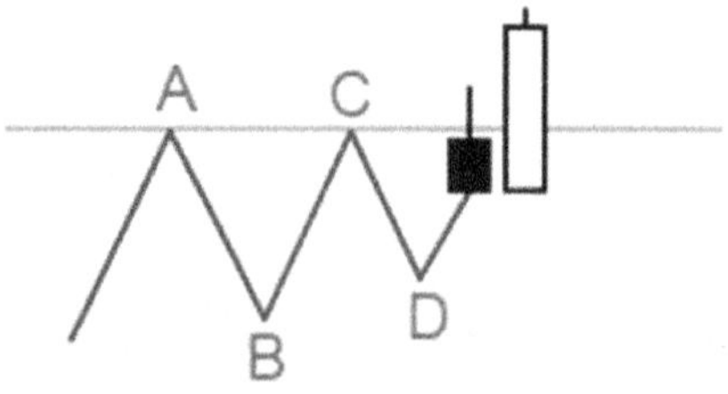

Figure 2.16: Breakout candle

If the wick is not excessively long, a break candle is considered strong when it breaks decisively and completely surpasses the previous wick's high. The reason is simple: the highest point of that wick still represents the zone controlled by the Bears — the area where they previously pushed price downward.

If the next candle breaks above the breakout level but does *not* clearly exceed the highest point of the previous candle's wick, the Bears still have room to counterattack and drive price back down.

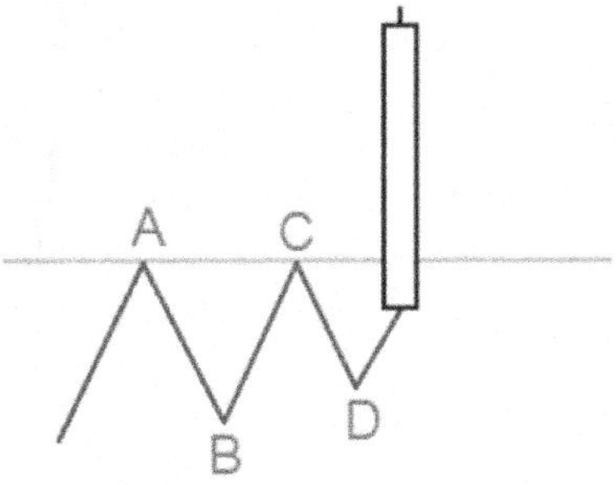

Figure 2.17: Breakout candle

Another situation traders should pay close attention to is when the breakout candle closes far above the breakout level. In this case, if you enter the trade right at the candle's closing price, the distance to your stop-loss becomes considerably large. This widens your risk and makes the R:R ratio far less attractive, while also increasing the likelihood that the price will retrace back toward the breakout level before continuing in the trend's direction.

As mentioned earlier, the ideal entry area is still around the breakout level itself, with the stop-loss placed below D — the nearest low of the pattern. When price breaks too far beyond the breakout level, entering immediately on that candle means accepting significantly higher risk without a proportional increase in potential reward.

From this, we can establish the third internal enhancer of the breakout model:

- The breakout candle should not have a long wick.
- The breakout candle should not close too far from the breakout level.

Figure 2.18: Breakout example

Figure 2.18 presents a case where the breakout candle has a long wick — a negative sign indicating weak breakout momentum. During this phase, the Bears attempted to push price beyond the breakout level, but the Bulls quickly counterattacked, forcing price back down and leaving a long upper wick. The struggle between the two sides continued in the following candles after the breakout, indicating that the market remained undecided. When such a strong tug-of-war occurs, the breakout loses reliability, and the likelihood of the price being pulled back to the previous range becomes quite high.

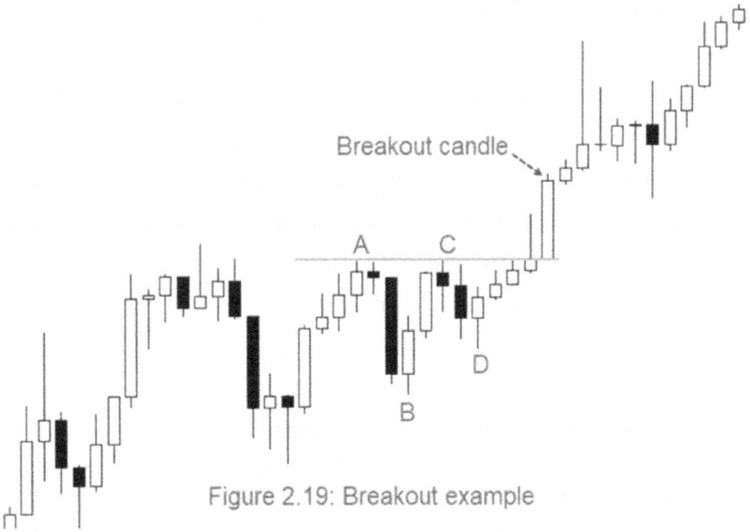

Figure 2.19: Breakout example

Another situation to watch out for is when the breakout candle has an overly long body. While this might appear as a sign of strong bullish momentum and a clear breakout by the Bulls, entering at the candle's closing price and placing your stop-loss below point D would create a wide distance between entry and stop — resulting in an unattractive R:R ratio. In this case, the price would need to travel a considerable distance to generate a reward proportional to the risk taken. There are two better ways to handle this scenario.

First, you can wait for the price to pull back toward the breakout level — a common retest area where price often revisits the recently broken resistance before continuing in the direction of the breakout. However, doing so also carries the risk of missing the trade entirely, as price does not always retest after breaking out.

The second option is to drop down to a lower timeframe to find an earlier entry. On the smaller chart, you can see the internal structure of the breakout move more clearly, identifying short pullbacks or smaller confirmation signals — such as candlestick formations — that allow for a better entry while maintaining the same breakout logic from the higher timeframe.

In short, a well-formed breakout candle is the key factor confirming a reliable breakout. It should clearly display the strength of the dominant side, have a solid body, close not too far from the breakout level, and have relatively short wicks. Conversely, breakout candles with long wicks or closing too far beyond the breakout point weaken the setup's quality. Once you learn to read the language of individual candles, you'll no longer see breakouts as mere "price movements," but as the visible expression of real strength driving the market's next move.

Internal Enhancer 4 – Price Compression

The next internal enhancer we'll explore is compression — also known as price accumulation before a breakout. This is the phase where market volatility gradually contracts, candles become smaller, and the distance between highs and lows narrows over time. On the chart, compression looks much like a spring being tightly coiled — the longer and tighter it's compressed, the stronger the release that follows.

In practice, most powerful breakouts are born after a clear phase of price compression. This is when both the Bulls and Bears are holding their positions, waiting for the right moment. At the same time, liquidity decreases and market energy quietly builds up. Once one side gains enough strength to break that balance, the price tends to explode quickly and decisively in the direction of the breakout.

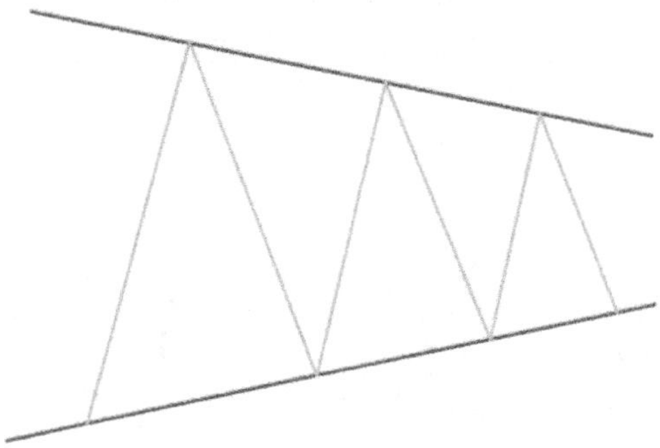

Figure 2.20: Price compression

Let's imagine a scenario where a strong bullish move pushes the price upward, followed by a bearish counterattack that drags it back down. Then, supported by the prior upward momentum, the Bulls return and push the price higher again. This back-and-forth struggle persists, causing prices to fluctuate within a defined range without decisively breaking in either direction. Over time, this tug-of-war forms a sideways consolidation. And if, during this phase, the supply and demand zones — the territories of the Bulls and Bears — start moving closer together, it means the price range is narrowing. This narrowing is the essence of **price compression.**

Price compression represents the market's process of accumulating energy. The Bulls aren't yet strong enough to break out, and the Bears lack the power to push the price lower. As the two forces move toward a state of near perfect balance, it takes only one side to tip the scale and the built up energy will be released all at once, creating a powerful and decisive breakout.

As the name implies, **price compression** refers to the tightening of price movement. If the price within a sideways range continues to fluctuate strongly, it signals that both sides are still actively contesting control — in that case, compression is weak. Conversely, when candles begin to shrink, wicks shorten, price swings narrow, and movement becomes more compact within a confined area, it indicates strong compression. At this stage, supply and demand are nearly balanced, liquidity declines, and pending orders start to accumulate on both sides of the market.

Figure 2.21: Price compression

Figure 2.21 shows a typical example of a price compression zone. In this case, we can clearly observe the characteristics of a healthy compression phase: small candles, gradually shortening candle bodies, shorter wicks, and highs and lows that move closer together over time.

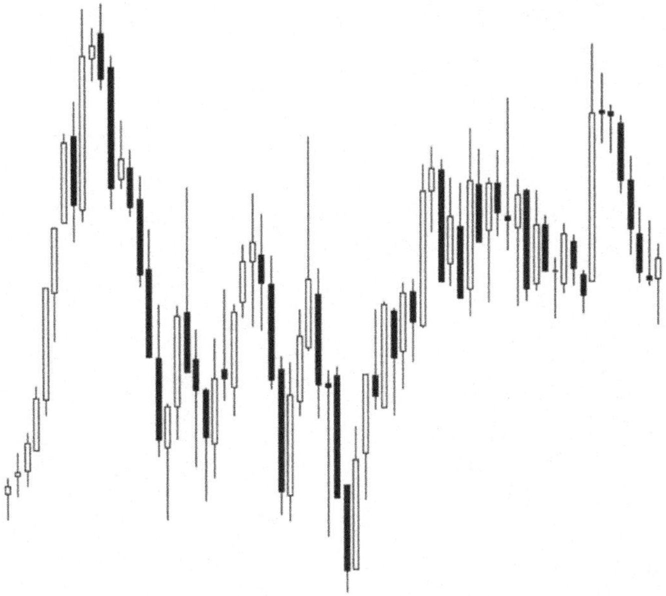

Figure 2.22: Sideways range

In Figure 2.22, although the price is also moving sideways, the level of compression is much weaker. A closer look reveals that the swings here have wide amplitude, the candles have large bodies and long wicks, and highs and lows form continuously. This indicates that the Bulls and Bears are still actively battling, and the balance between supply and demand has not yet been established.

Types of Price Compression

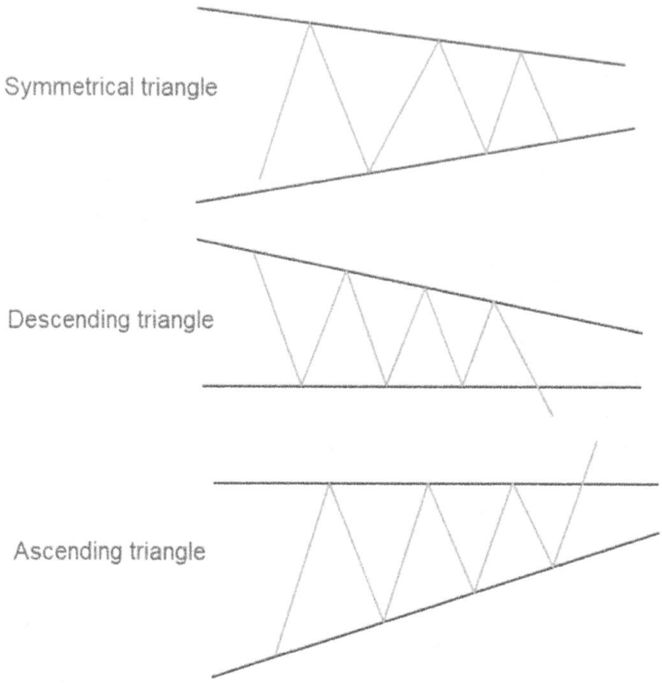

Figure 2.23: Types of price compression

It is this phenomenon of price compression that often forms triangle-like shapes on the chart — a direct result of both sides continuously narrowing their range of battle.

When the Bulls and Bears are in near-perfect balance, the price compresses into a symmetrical triangle, where highs gradually decrease and lows increase at roughly the same slope. This type of compression reflects intense indecision, with neither side holding a clear advantage.

If the Bears begin to dominate, the highs will consistently move lower while the lows either stay flat or rise only slightly. The pattern then forms a descending triangle — a sign of growing bearish pressure and a higher likelihood of a breakout to the downside.

Conversely, if the Bulls are stronger, the lows will continue to rise while the highs remain flat or decline only slightly, forming an ascending triangle. This indicates mounting bullish pressure and a greater chance of an upside breakout.

When trading the Breakout strategy, we'll look for these ascending and descending triangle formations as key structural setups aligned with the prevailing uptrend or downtrend.

Application of Price Compression

So, what does price compression actually bring to our model? Let's look at this phenomenon through the lens of the ongoing battle between the Bulls and the Bears.

Strong Price Movement

When price begins to tighten and move within a narrow range, it reflects that both sides — the Bulls and the Bears — are consolidating their positions and reinforcing their territories.

During this stage, the strength of the two forces is usually well balanced. Neither side is strong enough to take full control, so the price becomes "trapped" within a confined range. However, just like in physics, compressed energy cannot remain contained forever. Once the pressure from one side becomes strong enough, the balance breaks, and the price bursts forcefully in the direction driven by the dominant side.

You can imagine this like inflating a balloon — the more air you pump in, the greater the internal pressure becomes, until eventually, the balloon can no longer withstand it and bursts. The market behaves similarly: when a price has been compressed for too long, the subsequent breakout often comes with strong momentum and decisive movement.

Better Stop-loss Placement

Price compression not only provides a momentum advantage once a breakout occurs, but it also gives traders a safer stop-loss placement when entering in the direction of the breakout.

This is one of the clearest advantages of trading breakouts that form after a period of compression. When price has been tightly compressed within a narrow range and suddenly breaks out, entering at the breakout point typically allows for a tighter stop-loss — one that's also safer, since price rarely reverses sharply after breaking free from such a tight zone. The reason is simple: the market is already in its most "compressed" state, where both the Bulls and the Bears have exhausted most of their effort, leaving little room for deep pullbacks.

For instance, in an uptrend, you can place your stop-loss at the nearest low within the compression area, or at the previous low if the first one feels too tight. This closer placement helps you achieve a more favorable R:R ratio while maintaining strong protection for your trade.

Some traders believe that placing their stop-loss farther away makes their trades safer. Because of this, they often have the habit of widening their stop-loss whenever the price moves against them, or setting it too far from the high or low that the Bulls or Bears are likely to defend. This is a flawed mindset.

The reason is simple: when you place your stop-loss farther away, you're increasing the amount of risk per trade while simultaneously lowering your R:R ratio. To maintain a balanced R:R, you would need to expect the price to move significantly farther in your favor — a goal that is rarely easy to achieve. The market is full of short-term fluctuations that can test your patience and emotional stability long before reaching those distant targets.

Conversely, if you can identify a tight yet technically sound stop-loss — for example, just below a compression zone or the nearest support area — the distance to your take-profit target will also be shorter, making it easier to achieve. A stop-loss that is short, logical, and technically justified is far superior to one that's simply placed "far away for safety." In trading, real safety comes from managing risk effectively, not from giving your stop-loss extra room.

In summary, price compression is one of the most important factors that increases the success probability of breakout setups. When price compresses, it means the market is accumulating energy after a period of balance between buyers and sellers. The longer this compression lasts, the stronger and more decisive the breakout will be. Besides offering explosive momentum, compression zones also provide optimal entry and stop-loss positions — tighter, safer, and more efficient than those found in wide-ranging markets. Understanding how compression forms, recognizing genuine accumulation areas, and patiently waiting for the right breakout moment will allow you to trade proactively — with higher confidence and greater accuracy.

Pattern Within a Pattern

The next internal enhancer is the pattern within a pattern — a situation where a smaller breakout pattern forms inside a larger breakout structure. This factor is not as mandatory as the previous four enhancers, but when it appears, it significantly strengthens and adds confidence to your trade setup.

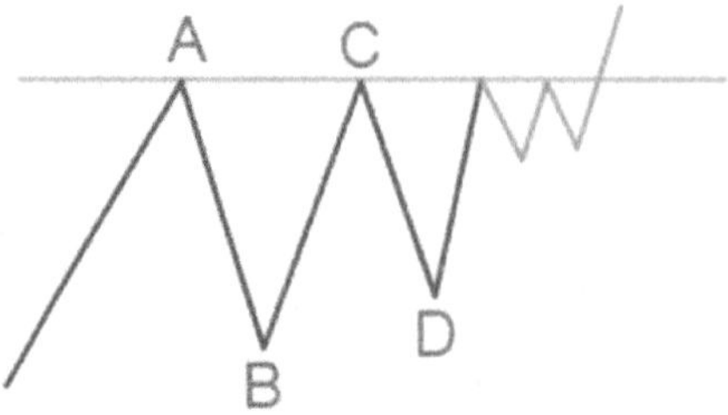

Figure 2.24: Double breakout pattern

The *"pattern within a pattern"* setup occurs when a smaller breakout formation develops around the breakout level of a larger pattern. For instance, in Figure 2.24 above, you can see a main pattern, followed by a smaller one forming right at its breakout level. In this case, when the price breaks through that breakout level, it effectively breaks out of *two patterns at once*. In other words, the breakout's strength is amplified.

One thing you'll immediately notice about this structure is the price compression that builds up within it — repeated selling attempts occur every time the price touches the breakout level. As we discussed earlier, the longer the compression, the stronger the eventual expansion will be. Therefore, a pattern within a pattern can be viewed as an advanced form of compression, adding extra power to the breakout that follows.

In some cases, the breakout candle that closes beyond the larger pattern's breakout level is clean and decisive, with price not moving too far away — giving you a great entry point that fits both patterns simultaneously.

In other situations, if you only wait for the breakout on the higher timeframe and encounter a long-bodied candle that closes too far from the breakout level, you might miss the trade when using a limit order. However, by observing the smaller pattern on a lower timeframe, you can often find a more optimal entry through the breakout candle of that smaller pattern — essentially an *early entry* within the larger structure.

This setup has been one of my personal favorites for years when trading the Breakout Strategy.

At this point, we've covered all four internal enhancers of the breakout model — the key building blocks that make an entry setup more structured, confident, and statistically favorable.

The first internal enhancer is the number of highs or lows, which reflects the level of effort the opposing side made before failing — the more equal highs or lows there are, the more reliable the breakout tends to be. Next comes the element of range, where we learn to assess the harmony of price swings within the pattern — a balanced, well-shaped range signals a healthier structure and a higher probability of success. The third factor is the break candle, the key signal revealing which side truly holds control of the market. Finally, price compression represents the buildup of market energy before the breakout — a tightly compressed structure often leads to a stronger expansion, offering traders the advantage of tighter, safer stop-loss levels.

Beyond these four core enhancers, there's one special additional factor — the *pattern within a pattern*. While it's not a mandatory condition, its presence is a strong positive sign. When a smaller breakout structure forms around the breakout level of a larger one, it shows that the market is compressing across multiple layers, building potential energy for a powerful move.

In summary, these four primary enhancers, along with the *pattern within a pattern*, provide a solid framework for evaluating the quality of any breakout setup. The more internal enhancers align, the higher your probability of success. In the next chapter, we'll move on to External Enhancers — the contextual factors that help determine *when* to take a breakout trade and *when* to stay patient and wait for a better opportunity. But before that, let's take a look at a few real examples — some with strong internal enhancers, and others without — to see how these principles apply in practice.

Figure 2.25: Breakout example

The pattern shown in Figure 2.25 is an example of what I would consider a beautiful case of **price compression**. The candles within the structure have relatively small bodies and short wicks, showing minimal volatility. Instead of forming clear waves, they tend to cluster tightly together — a classic sign of compression. In addition, the breakout candle itself is strong and decisive, breaking cleanly out of the pattern without closing too far from the breakout level. This combination creates one of the most attractive breakout setups — one that meets all four internal enhancers we've studied: multiple equal highs or lows, a well-balanced price range, a clean and powerful breakout candle, and solid price compression leading up to the move. It's precisely these kinds of setups that often produce the most reliable and high-probability breakout.

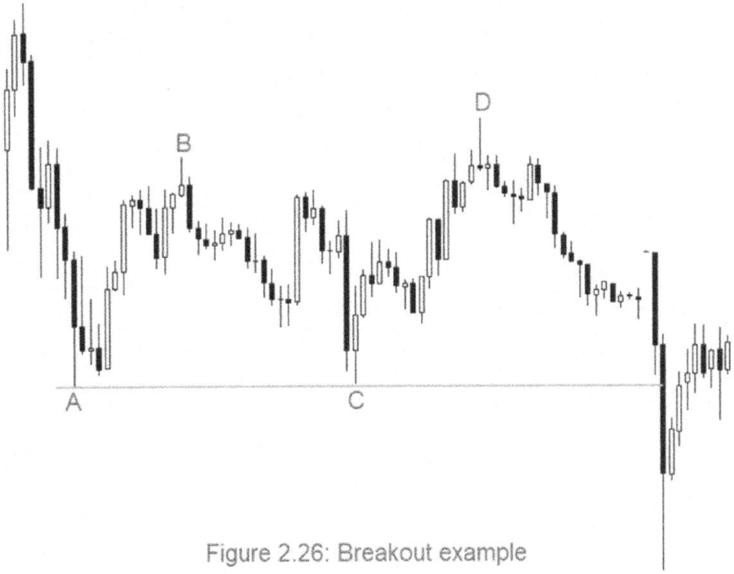

Figure 2.26: Breakout example

Figure 2.26 illustrates a breakout pattern that would be considered a weak setup.

First, point D lies outside the range of A–B. As mentioned earlier, when the price forms a high at D that exceeds the previous high at B and then breaks below the A–C axis, it indicates that the market has swept both the highs and lows. In many cases, this kind of price behavior leads to erratic movement within a sideways market that lacks clear structure. For that reason, I generally avoid trading breakouts with point D positioned in this manner.

Additionally, the swings between A–B, B–C, and C–D contain multiple smaller waves, indicating that buying and selling pressure is unevenly distributed. This imbalance makes the subsequent price movement less predictable. Furthermore, the degree of price compression is relatively weak in this example.

Another negative sign is that the breakout candle has a relatively long wick and closes noticeably far from the breakout level — a sign that the breakout lacks decisiveness and may be prone to reversal.

All things considered, I prefer to stay out of setups like this. While it's possible to win a few trades here and there with such patterns, they tend not to be sustainable or profitable in the long run.

CHAPTER 3: EXTERNAL ENHANCERS

Welcome to Chapter 3.

As we move into this chapter, we'll broaden our perspective beyond the breakout pattern itself to explore the external factors — the market conditions that directly influence the quality and reliability of a breakout.

If the internal enhancers help us determine whether a breakout pattern is structurally strong and technically sound, then the external enhancers tell us whether the *timing* and *market context* are right for taking the trade. In other words, this part helps you understand the *environment* in which your setup exists — because even the most perfect breakout pattern can fail if it appears in the wrong context.

In this chapter, we'll learn to recognize when it's time to follow a breakout and when it's better to stay on the sidelines. This is the step that turns a technically good setup into a truly effective trade — one that aligns with both structure and context.

External Enhancer 1 – Directional Wave

The first external enhancer we'll look at is the directional wave. This concept helps us understand the dominant movement of the market before a breakout pattern takes shape.

The directional wave acts like the main current of the market — it reveals which side currently holds control: the buyers or the sellers. When a breakout pattern forms in the same direction as the directional wave, the probability of success is significantly higher because we are trading *with* the prevailing market momentum. On the other hand, if the breakout pattern forms against the directional wave — meaning it moves counter to the market's dominant flow — then no matter how visually perfect the setup looks, the risk increases considerably.

In this section, we'll learn how to identify the directional wave and how to respond effectively to different market scenarios depending on its direction.

Definition of Directional Wave

A directional wave represents a strong and decisive movement in the market, often characterized by a steep slope and a series of candles moving in the same direction. These waves reveal which side — the Bulls or the Bears — currently holds control over the price movement.

Directional waves are what set trending markets apart from sideways conditions. In a sideways phase, price moves without a clear direction, forming alternating candles of different colors that reflect a lack of dominance from either side.

The Psychology Behind the Directional Wave

In a directional wave, the market demonstrates clear strength. Price moves swiftly, decisively, and with strong momentum in one direction, often covering a significant distance within a short period. This behavior reflects a collective psychological tilt in the market — either the buyers are filled with enthusiasm and continue pushing prices higher, or the sellers are in control, applying constant downward pressure.

In contrast, waves that are not directional tend to move more slowly and indecisively. They are made up of smaller, fragmented swings, with candles that have long wicks frequently sweeping through support and resistance zones. This price behavior reveals hesitation and a lack of consensus between the two sides of the market.

Figure 3.1: Directional Wave

Figure 3.1 illustrates typical bullish directional waves, shown as dashed lines. These waves consist of a series of consecutive candles of the same color, representing the dominant strength of the buyers. Between two directional waves, you can see a sideways range accompanied by price compression — a phase where price moves within an increasingly narrow range and lacks a clear slope.

A directional wave does not require every candle to be of the same color; however, when candles of the opposite color do appear, they are usually few in number and have small bodies. This indicates weak resistance from the opposing side, as the dominant force continues to control the market's momentum.

Trading with the Directional Wave

Supportive Directional Wave

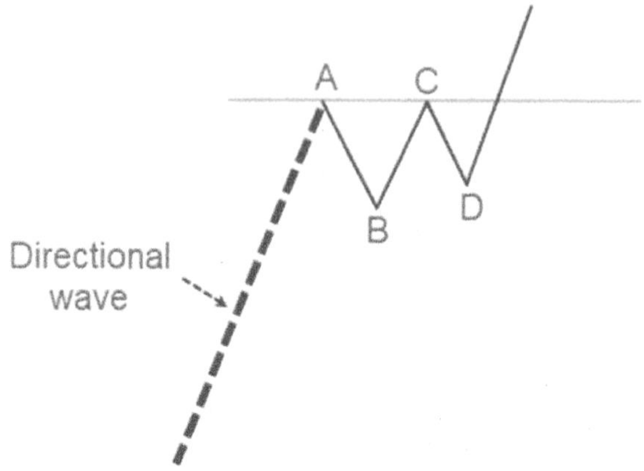

Figure 3.2: Supportive Directional Wave

Let's imagine a breakout pattern forming right after a wave that moves in the same direction — for instance, a bullish breakout setup appearing immediately after an upward wave. In this case, the pattern gains an additional layer of confirmation: the presence of a supportive directional wave.

This means you're trading in alignment with the prevailing market force, where the buyers are clearly in control. When a breakout pattern develops in the same direction as the directional wave, the probability of the price continuing along that path increases significantly. At this point, the market benefits from both momentum — carried by the supportive directional wave — and technical confirmation from the breakout pattern itself. Together, they create a powerful alignment between the larger trend and the breakout trigger, enhancing both conviction and reliability.

Opposing Directional Wave

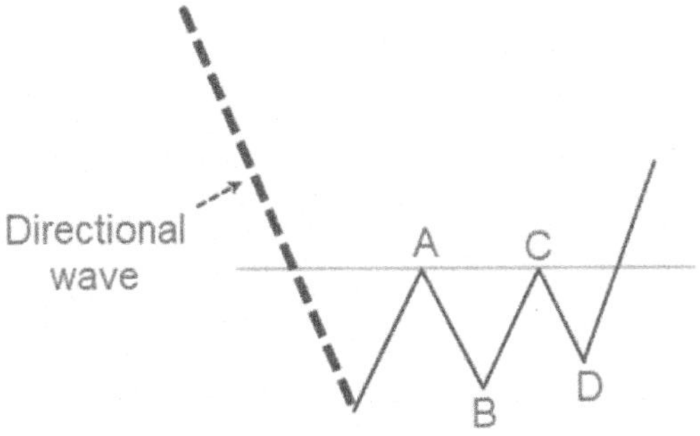

Figure 3.3: Opposing Directional Wave

Conversely, if this is a bullish breakout pattern but it is preceded by strong downward waves — in other words, opposing directional waves — then the setup faces an unfavorable condition. The presence of a prior bearish directional wave indicates that the Bears remain in control and have consistently pushed the market lower. Entering a buy position under such circumstances is like trying to fight against an army that already dominates the battlefield. The risk is significantly higher because the Bulls have yet to show any clear signs of regaining control or reversing the market's momentum.

A Directional Wave Followed by a Weak Pullback

The examples above illustrate directional waves that appear immediately before the ABCD breakout pattern. But what if the directional wave doesn't occur right next to the pattern — as shown in the illustration below?

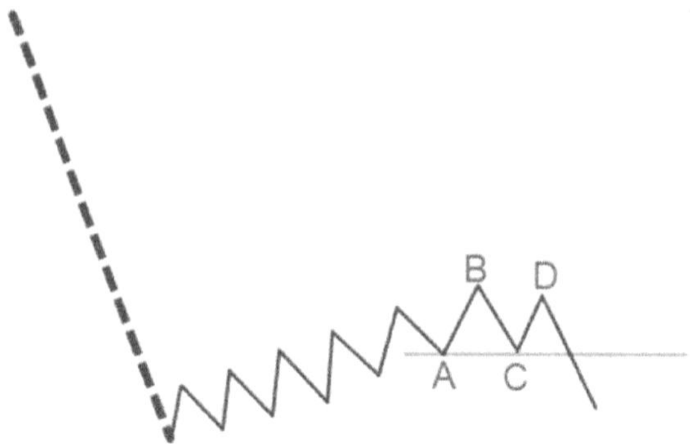

Figure 3.4: Supportive Directional Wave

In this case, the directional wave still qualifies as a supportive directional wave for the pattern.

Why is that? Although it doesn't appear immediately before the pattern — with a minor pullback occurring between the two — the pullback itself is shallow and lacks real strength. Therefore, it's unlikely that the selling pressure carried by the Bears from the previous directional wave has been neutralized. In other words, the bearish momentum from that directional wave still extends its influence over the pattern, thereby increasing the probability of a successful breakout.

A Directional Wave Followed by a Strong Pullback

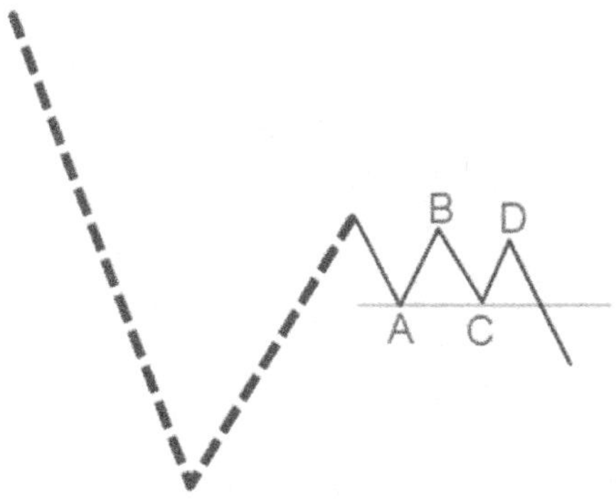

Figure 3.5: Conflicting Directional Waves

In this case, we have a bearish breakout pattern preceded by two types of directional waves: one strong bearish wave and one equally strong bullish wave.

This means the pattern is influenced by both a supportive element (the bearish directional wave) and a conflicting one (the bullish directional wave).

Such a setup reflects a market caught in strong contention between the two sides. The Bears have shown dominance through the initial downward wave, yet the Bulls have also proven resilient, pushing price upward with a steep and decisive move. As a result, market momentum becomes more balanced, making the upcoming breakout harder to predict.

Therefore, setups like this typically have a lower probability of success compared to patterns where the pullback (in this case, the bullish move) is not itself a directional wave. Generally, the fewer conflicting forces there are between waves, the more favorable the breakout setup becomes. But when both opposing waves are strong, the market environment turns more challenging, and entering a trade requires additional confirmation or alignment with other supportive factors to maintain safety and consistency.

Overextended Directional Wave

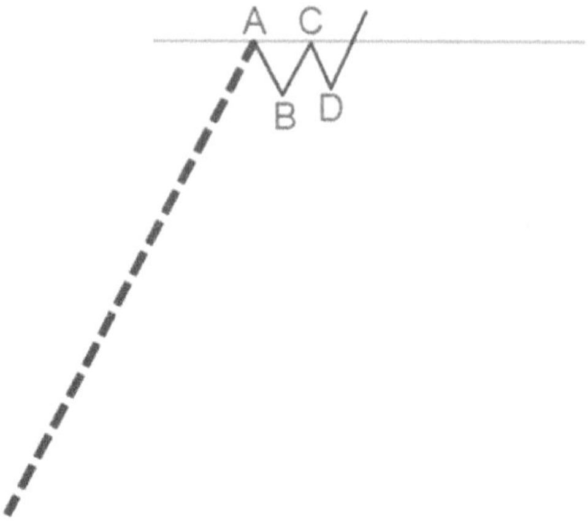

Figure 3.6: Overextended Directional Wave

Aside from the cases discussed above, there is another important scenario worth paying close attention to: when the price has already traveled too far in a major directional wave before the breakout pattern forms. In such situations, even if there is no clear resistance zone on the left, the price may still stall or even reverse.

The reason lies in market psychology. When the Bulls have pushed price too far in a strong upward move, buying power gradually weakens, as most existing buyers begin taking profits at higher levels. Meanwhile, new buyers hesitate to enter because they perceive the price as having "moved too far." At the same time, sellers start to show greater interest, as these higher price levels become attractive areas to open short positions. The result is a natural slowdown in bullish momentum and an increase in selling pressure — making breakout patterns that appear after an extended bullish wave more likely to fail.

An ideal directional wave is not excessively long, but rather short, steep, and powerful. In that case, the breakout pattern that follows is more supported. Shorter waves indicate that the market's momentum remains strong and not yet "exhausted," which increases the probability of a successful breakout.

In short, patterns that form after overly extended directional waves are generally less favorable, simply because the strength of the dominant side has already diminished significantly.

It's important to remember that a directional wave does not *guarantee* the next move in price — it merely increases the probability of success when the breakout aligns with its direction.

There will still be exceptions, such as cases where the opposing side gains enough strength to counteract the momentum of the previous directional wave, as shown in Figure 3.7.

In this example, there is no breakout moving in the same direction as the initial directional wave.

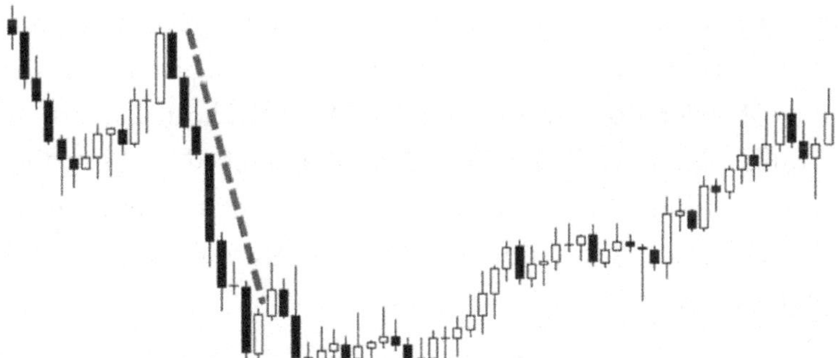

Figure 3.7: Directional Wave

Let's look at a few more examples of directional waves in combination with breakout patterns.

Figure 3.8: Supportive Directional Wave

In Figure 3.8, we have an ABCD pattern with a very well-defined price compression. Before the pattern formed, a directional wave was created, consisting of several bullish candles that clearly indicated the dominance of the Bulls. After that, the Bears counterattacked, halting the Bulls' advance and pushing the price down to B. However, the retracement wave had only a moderate slope, indicating that the Bears' counterforce was not particularly strong.

Ideally, the directional wave should appear immediately before the pattern, but this is not a strict requirement. As long as the wave is not too far away and there is no unfavorable market structure between the directional wave and the pattern, it can still be considered a supportive directional wave that increases the breakout's probability of success.

Figure 3.9: Supportive Directional Wave

In Figure 3.9, we see an example of a bearish directional wave. The breakout pattern is supported by a clear downward directional wave. Although there were some earlier bullish impulses, this directional wave decisively broke through the previous upward structure, signaling that the Bears have taken control of the market. As a result, the breakout pattern in this case is supported by the directional wave, which increases the probability of a successful trade.

In summary, the directional wave helps us determine whether a breakout pattern is moving in line with the prevailing market strength. When the pattern forms in the same direction as the directional wave, the probability of success is higher, since you are trading with the flow of momentum rather than against it. However, a directional wave alone is not a guarantee — it serves only as a supportive factor. Therefore, it should always be considered in combination with other enhancers to ensure safer and more effective trade execution.

External Enhancer 2 – Market Structure

The second external enhancer is market structure — one of the most fundamental elements for identifying the broader context in which a breakout pattern forms. Understanding market structure is like having a battlefield map before taking action. If a breakout pattern forms in alignment with the prevailing structure, it means you're moving with the natural flow of price. Conversely, if the pattern develops against the structure, you're essentially trading against the market's dominant direction — a situation that significantly reduces your probability of success.

In this section, we'll explore how different types of market structures can influence the outcome of a breakout trade.

Breakout Pattern Aligned with Market Structure

Figure 3.10: Supportive Market Structure

In Figure 3.10, a clear bullish market structure is evident, followed by a pullback where the price returns to a Bull Zone and forms a breakout pattern. The market may or may not display a directional wave before the pattern forms. Nevertheless, in this case, the breakout pattern aligns with the overall market structure, which is bullish.

In other words, the preceding market structure supports the upward movement, and the pattern itself is also backed by the Bull Zone. When the breakout occurs, it signals that the Bulls are stepping back in and taking control of the market once again.

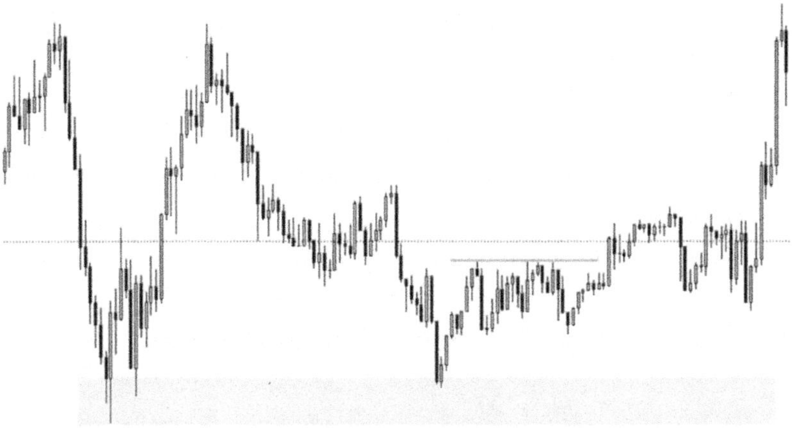

Figure 3.11: Supportive Market Structure

In Figure 3.11, a large Bull zone is illustrated on the chart. After a period of consolidation and back-and-forth between the two sides, the price pulls back into this area. Shortly afterward, a breakout pattern forms, and the price breaks above the breakout level. Supported by the strength of the prior Bull zone, the price clears the area of contention and continues to advance upward decisively.

Breakout Pattern Against Market Structure

Figure 3.12: Opposing Market Structure

In this case, we have a bullish breakout pattern forming within a bearish market structure. As a result, even if the price breaks above the pattern, the breakout may not be sustainable. From a broader perspective, the market is still under bearish control. Once price breaks upward, it is likely to encounter a Bear Zone above, where sellers may re-enter and push the price back down.

Situations like this are quite common. A breakout pattern only reflects short-term strength — the battle within its own boundary. However, if the larger structure remains bearish, the opposing pressure from the Bears is still dominant, making bullish entries prone to reversals. Moreover, when trading against the prevailing structure, the risk–reward ratio of the setup tends to worsen, as price often meets resistance above or reverses earlier than expected. In short, a bearish market structure does not support a bullish breakout pattern.

Breakout Pattern Within a Sideways Structure

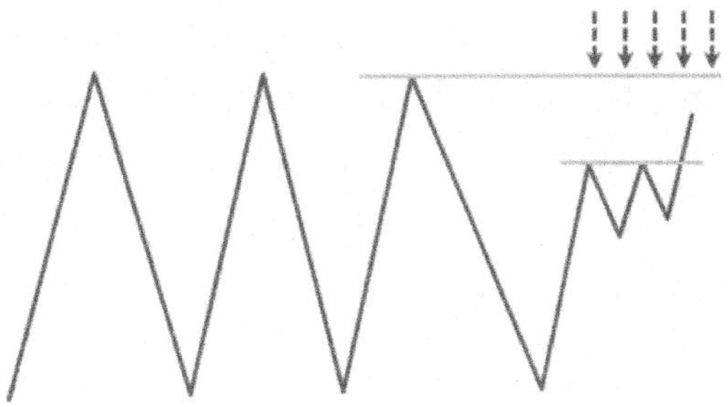

Figure 3.13: Sideways Market Structure

If a bullish breakout setup forms within a sideways market structure, as shown in Figure 3.13, the degree of support for the setup will largely depend on the risk–reward ratio.

Specifically, if the profit target lies near the closest Bear Zone but still provides a favorable risk–reward ratio — for example, 1.5R or higher — the trade can still be considered. However, if the pattern forms too close to the Bear Zone, the available space for the price to move upward becomes limited. In that case, sellers may quickly re-enter once the price reaches that area, causing the move to lose momentum and reverse after only a short advance.

Therefore, within a sideways structure, a breakout pattern only has an advantage if there is sufficient room for the price to move toward a reasonable target. Otherwise, nearby resistance levels can easily "suffocate" the breakout and significantly reduce its probability of success.

In summary, market structure provides the foundation for assessing the context in which a breakout pattern forms. A technically sound pattern that goes against the prevailing structure is like rowing against the current

— it can work, but it's harder and riskier. Conversely, when the pattern aligns with the broader structure, it benefits from the market's natural momentum, improving both its win probability and risk–reward ratio.

In some cases, a sideways structure can still be acceptable if the price has enough room to travel and the potential reward justifies the risk. However, if the pattern forms close to the boundary in the direction of the breakout, that boundary may quickly become an obstacle to price movement.

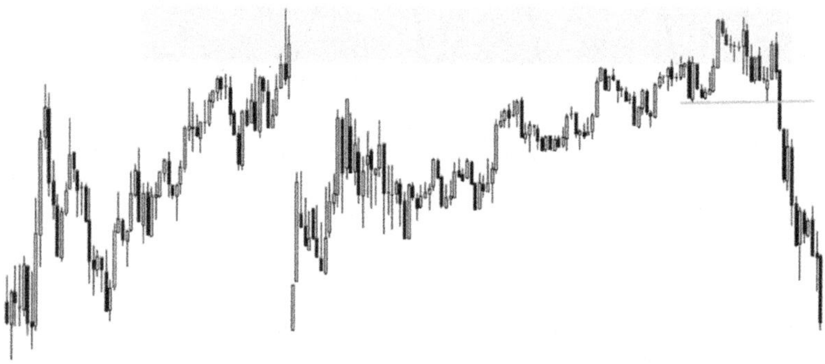

Figure 3.14: Supportive Market Structure

In Figure 3.14, we observe a wide-ranging sideways market. In the latest development, the Bulls attempt to counter the previous decline by gradually pushing the price up toward the Bears' key resistance zone. The Bullish waves show a moderate slope, indicating that the Bulls are not particularly strong in this Bull–Bear battle. Since the breakout pattern forms at the start of the Bearish wave and is supported by a nearby Bear Zone right above it, the momentum shifts entirely in favor of the Bears after the breakout. This is an example of a successful trade scenario within a sideways range, as the broader market still provides ample room for the price to move further in the breakout direction.

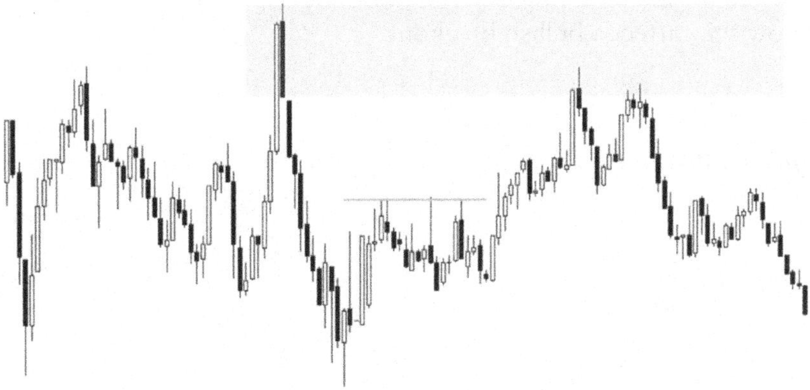

Figure 3.15: Unsupportive Market Structure

In Figure 3.15, we again see a sideways market with a breakout pattern forming within it. However, unlike the previous example, the position of this pattern leaves little room for the price to move after the breakout. As the price reaches the nearby Bear zone, the Bears quickly step in and push it back down. This represents a market structure that does not support the breakout pattern.

External Enhancer 3 – Support/Resistance

The third external enhancer is the support/resistance zone — one of the most fundamental yet highly influential factors affecting the effectiveness of a breakout pattern.

Simply put, a support or resistance zone represents a price area where either the buyers or the sellers have previously shown significant strength, causing the price to stall, reverse, or move sideways. These zones can appear above the current price (resistance), below it (support), or sometimes right around the breakout level itself. Depending on their position and context, they can either support or oppose the breakout setup.

In the following sections, we'll analyze each type of support/resistance and see how they affect a bullish breakout.

Upper Resistance

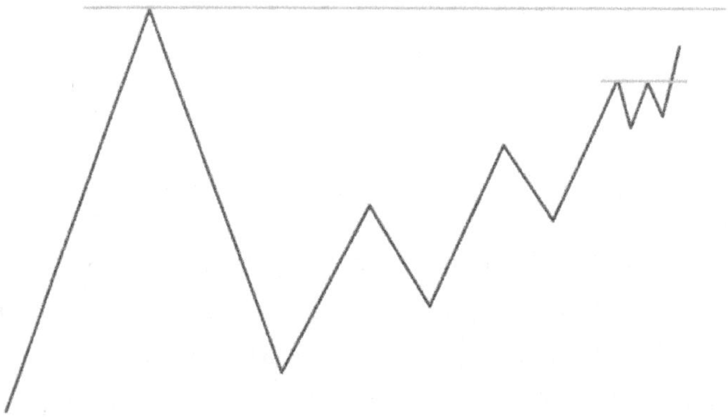

Figure 3.16: Upper Resistance

If a resistance zone — for example, a Bear Zone — is located right above the pattern, then when price moves upward and forms a breakout pattern close to that zone, it creates an unfavorable context for a buy setup. The reason is simple: although the entry and stop-loss points may follow the correct strategy, the distance to the major Bear Zone above is too short. This allows sellers to re-enter easily, pushing price back down after only a brief upward move. As a result, the breakout loses momentum and fails to travel far.

This situation is known as "nearby upper resistance" — meaning the resistance zone is positioned too close to the pattern, restricting price movement after the breakout. In such cases, the probability of price extending further is lower, and the risk–reward ratio becomes less attractive.

Of course, there are times when price breaks through the resistance entirely and continues to rally. However, recognizing such situations requires careful observation of candlestick behavior. If you see multiple bearish candles forming at the resistance, it suggests that sellers are stepping in aggressively. Conversely, if price cuts through the area with a strong sequence of bullish candles, that's a sign of a genuine breakout.

Still, according to the core logic of market behavior — the ongoing battle between Bulls and Bears — a nearby resistance zone is typically a non-supportive factor for a breakout pattern. With sufficient backtesting, you'll notice that the strongest and most reliable breakouts typically occur when the price has enough open space to move freely, without the immediate pressure of a nearby resistance zone.

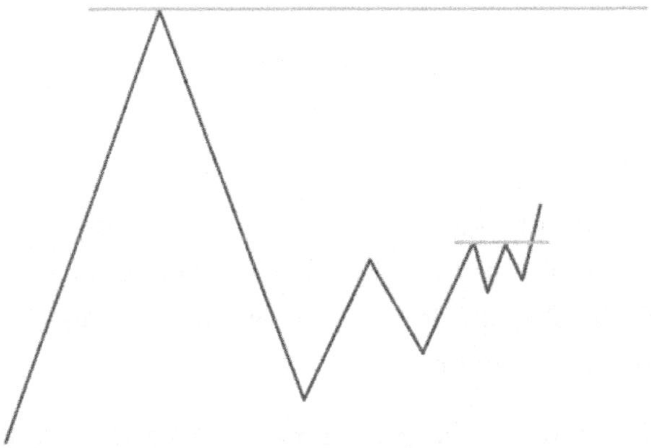

Figure 3.17: Upper Resistance

Another scenario involving upper resistance is when the resistance zone is located relatively far from the pattern, as shown in Figure 3.17. This is referred to as the **"distant upper resistancc"** casc. If a bullish breakout pattern forms below, with the resistance zone clearly separated by a noticeable gap, the trade setup becomes more favorable.

The reason is that the distance between the pattern and the resistance provides sufficient space for the price to move after the breakout. In this situation, entering at the breakout point and setting the stop-loss according to plan still allows the price enough room to develop in the breakout direction, maintaining an attractive risk–reward ratio.

Break-level Resistance

Figure 3.18: Break-level Resistance

Another scenario occurs when a major resistance zone coincides with the breakout level itself. In this case, if the breakout pattern forms right at that zone and price breaks upward through it, the resistance zone actually becomes a **supportive factor** for the pattern.

The reason is that when the price breaks above the breakout level, it simultaneously breaks through a key resistance area previously dominated by the Bears. That price level had long acted as an impenetrable stronghold for the sellers, one that the Bulls needed time and effort to approach again. Therefore, once price decisively clears that entire zone, it signals overwhelming buying strength and a clear shift in market control.

As discussed earlier, when one side fails repeatedly before finally succeeding, the eventual breakout tends to carry strong momentum. Hence, if a resistance zone aligns with the breakout level and is broken decisively, it no longer acts as an obstacle — instead, it becomes confirmation of the Bulls' victory. In this situation, the resistance zone transforms into a **supportive zone** for the breakout, reinforcing the probability that the price will continue to move strongly in the breakout direction.

Lower Resistance

Figure 3.19: Lower Resistance

In the third scenario, we have a breakout pattern with a support/resistance zone located below the breakout level. This setup also provides a **supportive context** for the pattern.

This is because, during the formation of the pattern, the market was moving sideways after reacting to that zone. At this point, a battle between Bears and Bulls takes place — the Bears attempt to push the price lower, while the Bulls defend the zone and try to drive it back up. When the price finally breaks above the breakout level, it signifies that the Bulls have won the battle and regained control of the market.

More importantly, because the support zone now lies below the price, it no longer acts as an obstacle; instead, it becomes a new **support base** for the price if a pullback occurs after the breakout. In other words, when the breakout level is positioned above a support zone, that zone helps reinforce the reliability of the breakout pattern and provides a safer stop-loss area.

As we conclude this chapter, it becomes clear that the external enhancers — including the directional wave, market structure, and support/resistance zones — form the *context* within which every breakout pattern must be evaluated. A pattern may look technically perfect, but if it forms against the prevailing wave, opposite to the market structure, or faces a nearby resistance zone, its advantage will be significantly diminished. Conversely, when a breakout pattern appears within a clear trend, supported by a directional wave, aligned with the broader market structure, and free from nearby resistance — that is when you have one of the highest-probability setups.

In other words, the breakout pattern is the *bullet*, while the three external factors are the *barrel*. Only when both are aligned can your shot be truly precise and powerful.

Now, let's go through a few examples to see how these supportive and unsupportive conditions play out in real market scenarios.

Figure 3.20: Breakout example

In Figure 3.20, we have a bullish breakout. Now, let's apply what we've learned to identify which factors are supportive and which are unsupportive.

Starting with the internal enhancers, we can see two supportive and two unsupportive elements:

- **Breakout level:** The line passes through two highs, but they are not perfectly aligned (High C is slightly higher than High A) — unsupportive.
- **Price range:** Balanced — supportive
- **Price compression:** Clear — supportive
- **Break candle:** The candle has a relatively long wick (about the same length as the body). In addition, the price movement from point D to the breakout occurs within a very narrow range, with several small-bodied candles showing no clear direction — indicating that the Bulls were not decisive enough in pushing the price upward — unsupportive.

Next, let's look at the external enhancers. In this case, we don't see any strong supportive factors:

- **Directional wave:** There are both supportive and opposing directional waves — neutral.
- **Market structure:** The breakout pattern is forming within a sideways market, leaving limited room for price movement — unsupportive.
- **Support/resistance:** There is an upper resistance zone located close to the breakout pattern. This resistance is strong, as the preceding bearish wave originating from it was steep — unsupportive.

To summarize, this setup includes four unsupportive factors, two supportive factors, and one neutral factor. Overall, both the internal and external conditions are not particularly favorable for this breakout pattern.

Personally, in my breakout trading approach, my priority is always to ensure that all internal enhancers are supportive before considering a trade. That's a principle I've followed for many years — and I'll share more about it later in this book.

For now, let's continue with another example.

Figure 3.21: Breakout example

In Figure 3.21, we have another bullish breakout pattern. Let's analyze both the internal and external enhancers to see whether this setup is truly ideal for trading.

Starting with the internal enhancers, all four are supportive:

- Highs A and C are perfectly aligned, forming a clear and reliable breakout level.
- The price range is balanced and well-structured.
- Strong price compression is present.

- The breakout occurs decisively, with a long-bodied candle whose close is not too far from the breakout level.

As for the external enhancers, the picture is less ideal:

- **Directional wave:** There is no supportive or opposing directional wave — neutral.
- **Support/resistance:** There is an upper resistance zone close to the breakout pattern. This resistance has medium strength, as the preceding bearish wave from that zone had a moderate slope. We can see that the Bears immediately reacted when the price broke out and reached the resistance area, creating a brief sideways phase before the price eventually pushed higher — unsupportive.
- **Market structure:** The price encounters a medium-strength Bear zone just above — unsupportive.

In summary, we have four supportive factors, one neutral factor, and two unsupportive factors. This means the setup is stronger than the previous example, as it contains more supportive elements and fewer unsupportive ones.

In the next part of the book, we'll move on to trade execution — how to enter and take profit effectively.

CHAPTER 4: ENTRY AND TAKE-PROFIT STRATEGIES

Welcome to Chapter 4.

In this chapter, we delve into one of the most crucial aspects of refining your trading system — fine-tuning entry points and determining take-profit levels.

After understanding the internal and external enhancers that influence the probability of a breakout's success, it's now time to put everything together and build a breakout trading strategy with truly high winning potential.

The entry point is where you start a trade; the take-profit level is where you finish it. These two points may seem simple, but they mark the difference between a systematic trader and an emotional one. The way you choose your entry can minimize risk and maximize reward, while the way you set your take-profit will reveal whether you are disciplined — or ruled by emotion.

Entry

The first part of this chapter focuses on the entry point — where every trade begins, and one of the most critical factors determining your win–loss ratio.

A well-timed entry does more than just reduce risk; it gives you a strong advantage in both R:R ratio and trading psychology. When you enter at the right moment, your trade not only becomes statistically stronger but also mentally easier to manage — because confidence comes naturally when you know you've entered from a position of strength.

Break Entry

In Chapter 2, we explored the concept of the Basic Break Entry — the first foundation for trading breakouts systematically. In this chapter, we'll refine that concept further, helping you build an entry model that's clearer, more consistent, and more reliable.

A Break Entry is executed at the closing price of the breakout candle, under the following conditions:

- The pattern must contain at least two equal highs or lows, representing a clear contest between the two sides.
- The breakout candle should not have a long wick, and its closing price should not be too far from the breakout level — this ensures a favorable R:R ratio.
- The pattern should have a balanced price range, with point D located in the lower half of wave A–B for a bullish breakout, or in the upper half of wave A–B for a bearish breakout — ensuring symmetry and logical stop-loss placement.
- The structure should show price compression, with few distinct swings during the accumulation phase before the breakout.

These are mandatory conditions — the non-negotiable foundation of every breakout trade. Other factors can be adjusted depending on your trading style, but missing any one of these four will significantly reduce your win rate.

All the conditions above are the internal enhancers you learned in Chapter 2. They reflect the *internal health* of the pattern — how strongly the market itself supports the breakout direction within its own structure. When all of these enhancers align, you already have a base probability of success above 50%.

Improving that probability further — to 60%, 70%, or even higher — depends on the external enhancers discussed in Chapter 3, such as directional waves, market structure, and support/resistance zones. You can also refine and personalize your rules through market statistics and backtesting, tailoring them to fit your own trading style and preferred markets.

Stop-Loss: The stop-loss (SL) should be placed below point D for a bullish breakout, or above point D for a bearish breakout. This marks the final boundary between supporting and opposing forces within the pattern. If price breaks through this level, it means the breakout structure has failed — and you should exit the trade to preserve capital.

Limit Entry

We previously mentioned the Limit Entry in Chapter 2, but in this chapter, we'll take a deeper look at *when* and *why* this method should be used. The distinctive advantage of a Limit Entry lies in its ability to let you enter a trade at a better price, effectively optimizing your R:R ratio.

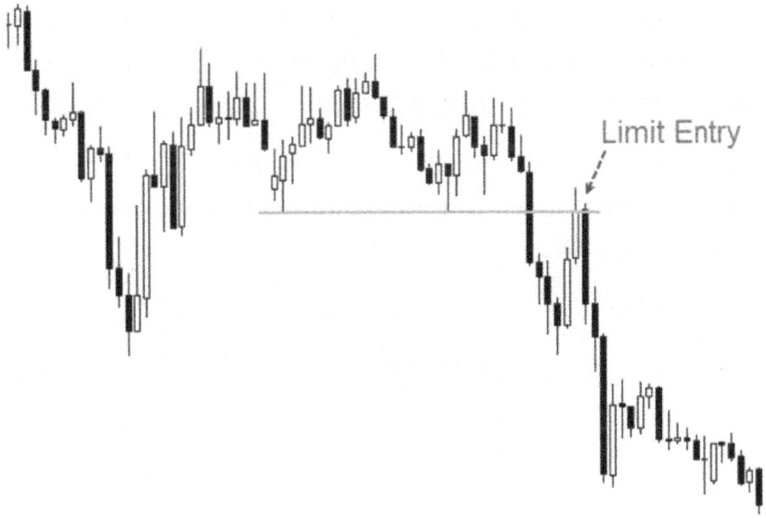

Figure 4.1: Limit Entry

In some cases, after price breaks through the breakout level, the market tends to make a slight pullback before continuing in the breakout direction.

When trading, if the breakout candle has already closed and the distance to your stop-loss (SL) isn't too far, you can confidently enter the trade right at the candle's close. However, for traders who want to optimize the R:R ratio, placing a limit entry at the breakout level is often a better choice. In this setup, if the price retraces to trigger your limit order, you'll enter at a more favorable price — shortening your stop-loss distance and improving your R:R. This allows you to reach your profit target faster (if you trade with fixed-R targets) or increase your overall R:R (if you trail profits dynamically).

The trade-off, of course, is that price won't always pull back to your limit level. In many cases, once the breakout happens, the market moves decisively in that direction — leaving your limit order unfilled. For that reason, the limit entry method is best suited for traders who are willing to miss some trades in exchange for a better R:R.

Regardless of which approach you choose, consistency is crucial. If you mix too many entry methods — sometimes entering at the close, sometimes waiting for a pullback — your system will lose its structure, and your decision-making will become clouded.

Pick one approach, test it, gather data, and commit to it. Only when your entry rule is consistent will you be able to evaluate the true effectiveness of your breakout strategy.

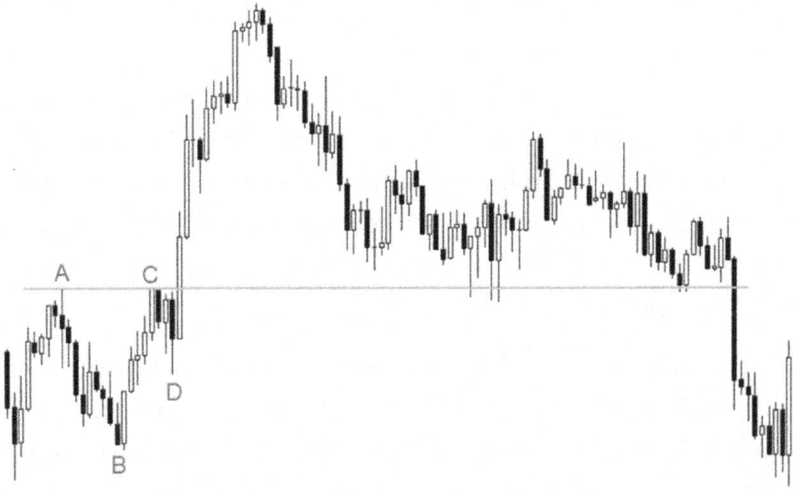

Figure 4.2: Unfavorable Limit Entry

A key note for those who trade using limit entries: you should only place a limit order when the breakout candle has just formed — not after the price has moved too far away from the breakout level.

For example, if the breakout candle has already pushed strongly upward and traveled far from the breakout level, and you then place a buy limit order at that level, the pullback that triggers your entry might actually be a strong selling move. In such cases, price may not simply pause at your entry zone but could break through previous Bull Zones entirely. This greatly increases your risk, as the market can shift from a bullish structure to a bearish one in just a single deep retracement.

Therefore, the rule is simple: only place limit orders when the price hasn't moved too far from the breakout level. If the price has already made a strong move, it's better to cancel your limit order to avoid being triggered during a corrective move dominated by the opposing side.

If you still want to trade in that area, wait for a clearer confirmation — such as a reversal candle or signs that the dominant side is regaining control. That way, your entry will have more supporting factors, and the area will serve as a more reliable buying zone.

Stop-loss placement follows the same principle as in the break entry method.

Ultimately, the entry point is the foundation of every breakout trade. Whether you choose a break entry or a limit entry, the most important thing is to follow your rules and remain consistent in your approach. A good entry doesn't come from intuition or luck — it's the product of confluence between price structure, candle behavior, and the supporting factors you've learned.

The break entry provides clearer confirmation from the market, while the limit entry allows you to optimize your R:R when the price retraces. Both methods have their pros and cons, but what truly matters is finding the one that best fits your trading style, then refining it through market statistics, backtesting, and real-market experience.

Take-Profit

After mastering the entry principles, the next crucial step is learning how to take profit — a process that may seem simple but directly determines your long-term profitability. A good entry is only the beginning; managing and exiting your trades at the right time is what allows you to preserve your gains and optimize overall trading performance.

Take-Profit Based on a Fixed R:R Ratio

My preferred and first method for taking profit is using a fixed R:R take-profit. That means when you enter the trade you already set the desired reward relative to the risk you accept.

For example, after you enter and place the stop loss below D, with a fixed R:R of 1:2, you measure the distance from the entry to the stop loss, then double that distance to find the take-profit level. When the price reaches that level, the trade closes automatically and the profit is preserved.

This method's advantages are simplicity, ease of tracking, and removal of emotional factors. You don't need to watch the market constantly or worry "should I hold or take profit now," because everything has been preset. Many traders refer to this as the "set and forget" style — place the trade, set the risk and reward, then let the market run.

Thanks to consistency and better emotional control, this take-profit style is very suitable for beginners or traders who want to train systematic trading thinking.

This method relies on a formula to beat the market. Therefore, there will be winning trades and losing trades, but the overall aim is to achieve a steady profit. The strength of this approach is discipline. There will be cases where the price nearly reaches the take-profit level and then returns to the stop-loss — we must accept that. There will also be cases where the price moves significantly, and we can't capture the full extent of the move. Still, sticking to the plan helps us avoid emotions and maintain stability in trading.

To trade this way, you don't immediately pick a fixed RR after learning the theory. After understanding the material, you should begin collecting statistics. Record every entry according to a fixed rule set. From that, measure how far the price runs when it goes as expected — what maximum RR it reaches and what the overall profit is at each R:R level. That lets you choose an appropriate R:R. I will explain the specific statistical steps in detail in later sections.

Flexible Take-Profit

The flexible take-profit method is designed for traders who prefer to closely monitor the market and aim to capture as much as possible from each price wave. Instead of fixing the take-profit point based on a predetermined R:R ratio, we observe the market structure's movement to decide when to exit. The advantage of this approach is that, in many cases, when a price breaks through a resistance zone and moves strongly, we can ride an extended wave, significantly boosting our overall profit.

However, flexible take-profit also carries certain risks. First, holding a position for too long can easily lead to emotional interference, especially when the price retraces midway. Second, this method requires the trader to have a solid grasp of market structure, be proficient in reading buying and selling pressure, and understand price reactions at key zones to identify the proper exit timing. Finally, since it requires constant monitoring, this approach can be time-consuming, especially for those who cannot stay in front of the chart regularly.

Partial Take-Profit

Another common take-profit method is the partial take-profit. This approach strikes a balance between safety and the ability to maximize profit. After price moves in your favor and reaches a certain level, such as 2R, you can close part of the position — for example, half — to secure some profit, while keeping the remaining portion open to capture further potential movement if price continues to trend strongly.

This method is especially suitable for traders who often struggle with hesitation: closing too early for fear of missing out, or not closing at all for fear of a reversal. Partial take-profit helps relieve that tension — it provides peace of mind by locking in profit while still allowing you to stay with the trend if the market continues to move favorably.

However, this method also has its own drawbacks. It requires you to monitor the market frequently and can easily lead to emotional swings — especially when you don't have clear rules on where to close the remaining portion. Many traders end up exiting too early or too late, reducing the effectiveness of the strategy.

Therefore, to apply partial take-profit effectively, you need to define two things in advance: the exact level where you'll close the first portion, and clear criteria for closing the rest. With a well-defined plan, this method becomes a powerful tool that helps you manage emotions while still taking full advantage of market opportunities.

In summary, there are three common take-profit methods: the fixed R:R take-profit, the flexible take-profit based on market behavior, and the partial take-profit. Each has its own strengths and weaknesses — no method is absolutely perfect. The right choice depends on your trading style, the time you can spend monitoring the market, and your level of emotional control.

If you prefer discipline and don't want to constantly monitor the chart, the fixed R:R take-profit will suit you best. If you're skilled at reading market structure and aim to maximize profit, the flexible take-profit offers greater opportunities. And if you want a balance between safety and potential, the partial take-profit is an effective choice.

Regardless of which method you choose, consistency is what matters most. Select the take-profit method that fits you, apply it long enough to gather clear statistical data, then adjust it gradually based on your own trading experience. When you understand the reasoning behind each take-profit decision, emotions will no longer control you — and that's when you truly take charge of your trading.

Why This Strategy

Many traders, especially beginners, often make a very common mistake: they try to learn too many patterns at once. Each pattern has its own logic, its own rules, and distinct price behavior. When you attempt to memorize and apply all of them simultaneously, confusion sets in — you no longer know when to enter or when to stay out. As a result, you fail to truly master any single effective method. Therefore, instead of chasing quantity, you should focus deeply on one pattern — in this case, the Breakout pattern — until you fully understand all its variations, confirmation signals, and possible failure reasons. Only then can you truly master a strategy.

The Breakout strategy is the best starting point because it is simple in structure yet clearly reflects the real strength of the market. In every breakout, we see a battle between buyers and sellers, where one side exhausts its strength and the other gains control. When price breaks through a key level, it's not just a line crossing resistance — it represents the outcome of a supply-and-demand battle, capturing the true essence of market movement. This method, therefore, helps you gain a deeper understanding of market structure and price behavior, rather than viewing the chart as a lifeless series of candles.

Typically, if the price truly moves in the right direction after a breakout, it tends to move decisively — fast and clear. We don't need to wait long, because there are usually few significant barriers ahead to slow the price down. This is one of the key advantages of the breakout pattern: it capitalizes on the moment when the market has just confirmed its direction, and the momentum of the dominant side is still at its strongest.

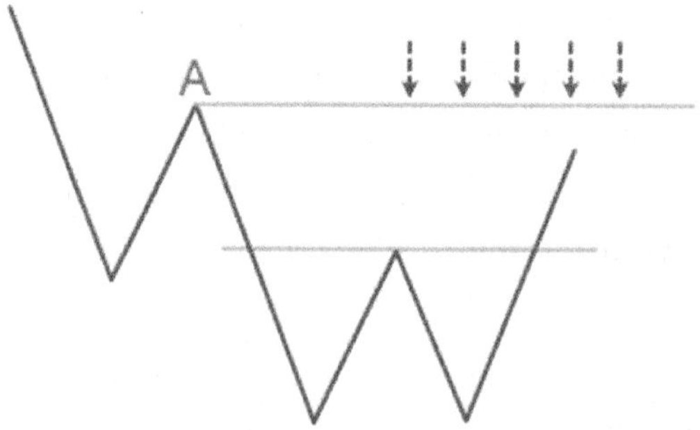

Figure 4.3: Double bottom pattern

If you compare it with traditional reversal patterns such as the double bottom, you'll see a clear difference. In the double bottom pattern, there is always a strong preceding downtrend, and the Bears still maintain control around previous highs — the resistance zones formed during the decline. When price retraces upward and forms two lows, as it approaches those highs (for example, high A in Figure 4.3), the Bears can easily step in again to push price down. This often causes the double bottom pattern to fail or move sideways for an extended period before a true reversal takes place.

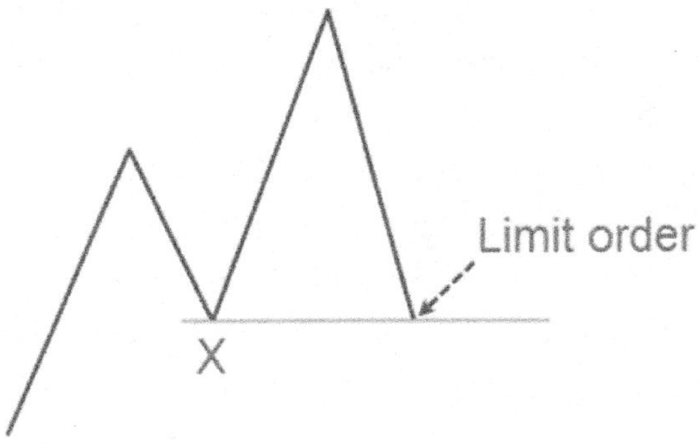

Figure 4.4: Unconfirmed Limit Order

Similarly, if we identify a strong key level — for instance, level X as shown in Figure 4.4 — and decide to place a buy limit order right at that zone without waiting for any confirmation signal, we are essentially entering a trade against the current market flow. This is particularly risky when the Bears have been in control, driving price downward with a steep slope, as selling pressure remains strong in such a context. Entering a buy limit under these conditions is no different from trying to "catch a falling knife." In other words, we are acting without any evidence that the selling side has truly lost momentum or that the buyers are ready to regain control.

In some cases, price may indeed bounce precisely from your limit zone and generate a profit. However, in the long run, if you trade based purely on luck like this, the risk of being attacked by the opposing side is extremely high. The position can quickly fall into a losing state as the market continues in its original direction before an actual reversal takes place.

Some traders, when first getting familiar with the breakout pattern, may feel that it looks quite similar to familiar formations like the triangle or the rectangle pattern. Indeed, the rectangle pattern is essentially formed when prices create at least two equal highs and two equal lows, resulting in a horizontal consolidation range that resembles a rectangle. However, the key difference lies in how we approach and apply it.

If you rely only on the shape without a clear set of entry rules, you'll almost certainly misidentify patterns once you step into real market conditions. The reason is simple — the market never moves as "cleanly" as it does in textbooks. Countless structures look *almost* like rectangles, but without clear criteria to distinguish good setups from bad ones — such as compression, the position of point D, the prior structure, or the behavior of the breakout candle — you'll likely end up choosing low-probability setups without even realizing it.

As a result, traders lose confidence in their own method, unsure of when to enter and when to exit. That hesitation doesn't come purely from emotion — it stems from not having a well-defined system of rules for making decisions. Therefore, what truly matters in trading isn't whether a pattern looks "perfect" in shape, but whether it has enough supporting factors behind it.

An effective trading method is never built on a single entry point. It's a combination of multiple factors — internal enhancers such as price compression, balanced price range, breakout candle, or breakout structure; and external enhancers such as the directional wave, market structure, or support/resistance. Each factor acts like a "brick" that helps build a solid foundation for your entry. The more supporting factors you have, the higher the probability of success.

That's why the breakout model you're learning in this book isn't just a "triangle" or "rectangle" pattern in appearance. It's a structured system with logic and clearly defined rules — rules that have been tested and refined through thousands of past trades. Once you understand and adhere to them, you'll no longer rely on guesswork, but instead make decisions with confidence, consistency, and discipline — the qualities every professional trader strives for.

In the next section, we'll dive into the most crucial and personally meaningful part of this book: method validation and risk management. This process bridges the gap between theory and real-world performance, transforming you from a learner into a market analyst — someone capable of spotting valid patterns quickly and accurately.

CHAPTER 5: METHOD VALIDATION & RISK MANAGEMENT

In this chapter, you'll learn how to validate your trading method and understand the critical role of risk management. Even if you've mastered the pattern, recognized the supporting factors, and know how to enter and exit trades, your method remains a matter of belief unless it's validated through data. The market doesn't care what you believe — it only responds to probabilities. And to uncover those probabilities, you must test your method through real statistics.

This chapter is divided into two main parts: method validation (which includes Market Statistics and Backtesting) and risk management. These two elements are closely connected — one helps you understand the actual probability of your method, while the other helps you turn that probability into sustainable long-term profit.

In short, Chapter 5 is where science meets reality. It's the point where your trading approach evolves from an interesting idea into a system that can be operated, verified, and proven profitable. This is the transition from *learning trading* to *doing trading* — a boundary few traders ever cross, but reaching this point means you're ready.

What Makes a Good Trading Method?

Welcome to the most important chapter of this book!

Yes — you read that right. *This* is the most important chapter, not the ones about patterns, entry strategies, or take-profit methods. Everything you've learned so far — from reading market structure, identifying Bull and Bear zones, to executing breakout trades — only becomes meaningful once you know how to validate, manage, and sustain your method in real trading conditions.

Before we go any further, let's start with a simple question:

Between these two options, which one would you choose?

(1) A system that delivers steady, consistent, and sustainable profits month after month.

(2) A strategy that can make you rich very quickly — but could also wipe out your account in just a few trades.

I believe most people would choose the first option — because no one wants to live in constant anxiety, making money one day only to lose it all the next. Yet in reality, the majority of traders out there act in the opposite way. They chase "explosive" setups, craving those big wins, the thrill of doubling or tripling their accounts — without realizing that the profit screenshots they see online are just the surface. Behind those snapshots could be long strings of losses that never get posted.

The truth is this: anyone can make money in the market, but very few can keep it over the long run. The financial markets don't reward those who win fast — they reward those who stay consistent, trade with a system, and know how to manage risk.

Probability in Coin Tossing

Let's play a quick game.

You have a coin — one side heads, one side tails. The rule is simple: if it lands on heads, you win $1.50; if it lands on tails, you lose $1.

Now here's the question: would you play if you only had $1 in your pocket?

The answer, almost certainly, is no. Because with just $1, you'd be risking your entire capital on a single 50–50 outcome. One unlucky toss and you're broke. On paper, the game looks "fair," but with such a small bankroll, the risk simply isn't worth it.

But what if I told you that now you have $100?

That changes everything. You can toss the coin 100 times — meaning you have 100 chances for statistical probability to play out.

If each toss has a 50–50 chance of landing heads or tails, then over 100 tosses you can *expect* roughly 50 heads and 50 tails.

- 50 wins: 50 × $1.50 = $75
- 50 losses: 50 × $1.00 = $50
- Average profit = $75 – $50 = $25

In other words, with a large enough number of trials, probability starts working in your favor — and that's exactly how professional trading works.

In other words, on each coin toss you have an average edge of $0.25 — that's $25 divided by 100 tosses.

If you look at a single toss, the outcome is pure luck — win or lose, it's random. But when the number of tosses increases, your statistical edge begins to show its power. And that's the core principle of trading: you don't have to win every trade — you just need a repeatable statistical edge that plays out over time, so that the average result tilts in your favor.

When the number of coin tosses is small, your results are almost random. You might win more or lose more, purely because of short-term luck. But as the number of tosses grows — hundreds, even thousands of times — statistical probability starts to reveal its true nature. The ratio of heads to tails gradually balances around 50%. And even with only a 50% win rate, you're still profitable, because your average win is larger than your average loss.

This is a crucial concept — it reflects the true essence of trading: you don't need to win often, you just need to win enough — and win bigger when you're right.

In this example, you're risking 1R to target a reward of 1.5R — or in trading terms, an R:R ratio of 1:1.5.

Now, the real question is: in trading, how can we build this kind of win–loss structure? How do we make sure that when we lose, we only lose 1R — but when we win, we can capture 1.5R, 2R, or even 5R?

Probability in Trading

The answer, as you may have guessed, lies in using stop-loss and take-profit orders. These two seemingly simple tools are what turn a random game into a system with a positive statistical edge — one where you don't have to win every trade to achieve consistent long-term profitability.

The process is straightforward: every time you enter a trade, you must cap your potential loss at a fixed amount — for example, 1% of your account, or $50, or $100 — depending on your capital size and risk tolerance. In contrast, your potential reward for each trade should be at least 1.5 times greater than that risk. In other words, if you lose, you lose $1; if you win, you gain $1.50. Simply by maintaining this rule, you already have a statistical advantage on your side.

Unlike a coin toss, trading is not purely random. You can increase your win rate above 50% by understanding price behavior, recognizing breakout patterns, and reading market structure and support/resistance zones — all the concepts we've covered in previous chapters. Each time you identify the right entry point — where the Bulls or Bears are about to lose strength — you're shifting probability in your favor.

When you fix the risk for every trade, you eliminate the fear of blowing up your account from one unlucky "coin toss." And when you aim for a minimum profit target of 1.5R or higher, you ensure that even with a win rate slightly above 40%, you can still achieve consistent long-term profitability.

Of course, in the short term, your results will still contain an element of randomness — you might experience a streak of consecutive losses or a string of wins. But over the long run, after hundreds of trades, the law of probability and sound risk management will naturally pull your results toward profitability.

These principles form the core mindset that allows us to determine whether a trading method is truly effective — whether it can produce consistent profit over time, or if its success is merely the result of short-term luck.

When people first start learning about trading or investing, most turn to the internet searching for "trading methods," "stock trading strategies," or "crypto trading systems." And what they find are hundreds, even thousands of different methods — from indicator-based strategies and automated robots to price action or volume profile approaches.

The problem is that everyone talks about having a *method*, but very few discuss having a *formula for consistent profit* — or how to verify that a method actually works. As a result, many beginners get lost in the maze of endless strategies, instead of realizing that the key question is not *"Which method wins?"* but *"Which method can be verified, has a positive expectancy, and can be executed with discipline?"*

In truth, success in any field can be broken down into two simple steps:

- Step 1: Have a method or formula that has been tested and proven to work.
- Step 2: Follow that method.

The Criteria of a Good Trading Method

Once you've understood the two fundamental steps above, it's time to look at the method itself. No matter which approach you choose, it must satisfy three key criteria.

First, does the method reflect the true nature of the market? In other words, does it capture the real dynamics of buying and selling — the constant battle between the Bulls and the Bears — or is it just a collection of arbitrary lines and random signals? A good trading method must always be rooted in actual price behavior and the psychology of market participants.

Second, are the entry and exit rules of the method clearly defined? A method only becomes truly effective when it is transformed into a concrete rule set, with specific points, such as when to enter, when to stay out, when to take a profit, and when to set a stop-loss. The clearer the rules, the less distracted you become. Trading is not about predicting the market — that's impossible — it's about following your rules under every condition.

Third, does the method allow you to achieve consistent profitability? Specifically, do its win rate and R:R ratio combine to create a positive expectancy? This cannot be guessed or assumed — it must be verified through statistics, by testing hundreds or even thousands of trades to see the real numbers. If a method cannot be proven with data, it remains nothing more than a belief.

When a method meets all three of these criteria, you no longer need to "guess" the market's direction. Instead, you simply follow the system and let probability and discipline do the rest.

The upcoming sections of this chapter are the ones I want you to truly invest your time in — not just to read, but more importantly, to *practice.* Only by analyzing market statistics and backtesting can you truly understand the nature of your method and determine whether it can deliver consistent profitability.

Note: For beginners, backtesting is a tool that allows you to test your trading strategy using historical price data. You can rewind to any point in the past, observe price movements as if they were happening in real time, and control the playback speed to go faster or slower as you wish. You'll also have a demo account to place trades, just like in live trading. During the process of refining your method, use backtesting to verify your rules. You can add elements that enhance your entry quality and remove those that decrease your chances of success. Each time you make an adjustment, test it again with data until you develop a system you truly trust.

Market Statistics

Market Statistics: The Starting Point

One of the most common mistakes traders make is rushing to backtest — or even trade live — just hours after learning a new method. They're eager to test the system as quickly as possible, believing that practice alone will bring understanding. But the outcome is usually the opposite: misidentified patterns, broken rules, and a poor sense of market structure.

I've met many traders like this. They're motivated and hardworking, but they start in the wrong order. They spend dozens of hours backtesting and meticulously recording data, only to realize later that much of their data is unreliable — because they didn't truly remember or understand the key elements of the pattern in the first place. Without a solid foundation, every backtest that follows becomes meaningless.

That's why before you backtest or trade live, the first thing you need to do is *analyze market statistics.* This is the stage where you observe, record, and analyze market price behavior according to a specific set of rules to identify recurring patterns with high probability. In other words, this is where you train your trading eye — sharpening your ability to recognize patterns, identify confirmation factors, and measure the real-world performance of your method.

Why Should You Analyze Market Statistics Before Backtesting?

The reason is that the nature of backtesting is completely different from market statistics.

When you backtest, you pick a point in the past and let the chart play forward without knowing what happens next. It's a practical exercise, but if you're not yet familiar with the model, it's easy to get confused and misread setups.

For most traders, finishing this book doesn't automatically mean remembering every concept, every internal and external enhancer, or all the possible variations of each factor. You'll still be navigating through a complex maze of candles, watching the constant battle between Bulls and Bears. That's why spotting clean, high-quality patterns quickly and accurately — the way experienced traders do — isn't something that comes right away. And if you've been trading with other methods for a while, you'll likely need to realign your mindset and market perspective to fit this new approach.

That's why the most important thing after finishing this book is to get familiar with the model by watching how price truly moves in real market conditions. The *Market Statistics* process is what helps you do exactly that.

In short, market statistics must come before backtesting, and backtesting must come before live trading. This is a natural progression — from observation to execution — helping you build a solid foundation before stepping into the real market.

How to Analyze Market Statistics

Model Used: Breakout Model & Internal Enhancers

At this stage, only scan breakout patterns that meet all internal supporting factors. You're still in the phase of getting familiar with the market, so don't overcomplicate things by mixing in external factors just yet. We'll integrate the external elements later, but for now, focus solely on collecting statistics for setups that satisfy the internal conditions of the breakout model.

Choosing the Market and Timeframe

You can apply this process to any type of asset — crypto, stocks, or forex. Choose the pairs or symbols you normally trade, and use the timeframes you're most familiar with. The more data you collect, the better.

Number of Trades to Record

At least 100 trades. The more trades you record, the more insights you'll gain — helping you refine and improve your trading setups later on.

Capturing Trade Images

When you spot a valid pattern (one that meets all internal enhancers), take a screenshot of the entry setup. Save the image and paste it into the *Image* column of your Validation Template — regardless of whether the trade later results in a win or a loss. This simple step is far more valuable than it seems. Over time, as you collect more data, each image becomes a visual record that reflects real market behavior — helping you understand how valid setups actually look and evolve in practice.

Recording, Categorizing R:R, and Selecting the Ideal R:R Level

Start by identifying your entry points (I recommend using the Break Entry setup for easier tracking), setting a stop-loss, and observing how far the price moves in terms of R before making a strong pullback. Round the number of R and record it in your Validation Template. The purpose of this process is to discover, over time, which R:R levels have the highest win probability and what the overall profit would be if you applied each level consistently. This allows you to choose a fixed take-profit ratio based on real data — not guesswork.

Any trade that reaches 1R or more is considered a winning trade. Trades that hit the stop-loss are considered losing trades.

You'll categorize the R results of your winning and losing trades according to these principles:

- **Group 1:** Winning trades supported by at least one external enhancer → include their R results.
- **Group 2:** Random wins — trades that violated three external enhancers but still won → exclude their R results (they don't represent long-term consistency).
- **Group 3:** Losses caused by normal market fluctuation (even though most internal and external enhancers were followed) → exclude their R results (these trades are part of the statistical variance).
- **Group 4:** Losses caused by not following at least one external enhancer, or by other factors you believe should be added to improve the method → include their R results.

An important note: when compiling your statistics, always *accumulate* higher-R trades into lower-R categories. For example:

- A trade that reaches 3R is also counted in the 2R and 1R groups.
- A trade that reaches 4R includes the 3R, 2R, and 1R groups as well.

After compiling all R results, calculate the total profit (**in R**) at each level:

- With an R:R ratio of 1:2, what's your total profit after 100 trades?
- With 1:3, 1:4, 1:5, and so on — what's the total profit after 100 trades?

From there, you'll identify which R:R ratio provides the best overall return — the optimal ratio for your trading system — and apply that R:R as your fixed take-profit target going forward.

Note: Some of you may be used to using a flexible take-profit approach rather than a fixed one. With this style, you determine your take-profit level based on the price action on the chart, which makes it harder to quantify the results. In this book, however, I'll focus on demonstrating how to collect statistics for a trading method that uses a fixed R:R *take-profit. This is the approach I've personally used for many years, and it's the one that fits most traders best.*

Trade Notes

This is the most important step in the entire market statistics process. It begins with recording both the supporting and non-supporting factors for each trade — including internal and external enhancers. Every time you write these notes, you deepen your understanding of the trading method and gain insights into which elements positively or negatively affect a trade at the moment you take it. Your system, in fact, is built during moments like these.

For example, if you notice a resistance zone above your buy setup, and after entering the trade, the price reverses from that zone, you would record in the "Non-Supporting Factors" column: *Resistance zone right above entry.*

Or, if your setup is supported by a directional wave and a bullish market structure, you would record in the "Supporting Factors" column: *Directional wave and market structure support the buy trade.*

Refining Your Entry Setup

At this stage, you compile all the data from your notes — specifically from the "Supporting Factors" and "Non-Supporting Factors" columns — to develop the most effective version of your strategy. You can write down the rules you plan to apply in your trades and place them somewhere visible at your workspace as a daily reminder.

For example:

After enough observation, you might notice a recurring pattern — most failed trades occur near strong support/resistance zones. At that point, you can add a new rule to your system:

"Avoid entering trades near strong support or resistance zones."

Or perhaps, during sideways market conditions, you find that your losing rate increases noticeably. The reason is that when the market moves sideways, neither side is clearly in control, making the pattern less reliable. After collecting enough data, you may conclude another important rule:

"Do not trade when the market is in a sideways condition."

As you collect more data, you'll gradually refine your set of rules until you feel comfortable and confident with it. The key is that this refinement is built on historical data — not personal bias or gut feeling. That distinction is critical.

Another point to consider is how *tight* your rule set should be. Depending on your trading style, you'll decide whether to apply every rule strictly or allow some flexibility. In practice, what works perfectly for one trader may not suit another.

The tighter your rules, the more selective your entries will be — which usually means a higher win rate but fewer trades overall. On the other hand, if your rules are looser and you skip some conditions, you'll get more trade opportunities, though your win rate might drop slightly.

So, ask yourself: which style suits you better??

- If you prefer fewer but higher-quality entries — you'll want a tighter rule set, only taking the best setups.
- If you prefer a more active trading style, you can adopt a more flexible rule set, accepting a bit more risk in exchange for higher trade frequency.

Market Statistics Templates

I've prepared two ready-to-use templates for tracking Market Statistics—feel free to make a free copy and start using them right away!

Market Statistics 1: Trade Statistics - at **shorturl.at/IdLeE**

Market Statistics 2: Determining the Optimal R:R Ratio - at **shorturl.at/4xcSQ**

Updating and Refining Your Trading Rules

Your rule set is not something fixed or permanent. The market changes, and a skilled trader must learn to adapt. Over time, you can refine your method to make it more efficient and better suited to your trading style. However, this doesn't mean you should constantly make adjustments. Once you have an effective set of rules, only make changes when there's clear, data-driven evidence that a modification is truly necessary.

Apply your rules in real backtests across different asset types to verify their consistency. If the results remain stable and the win rate meets your expectations, keep them as they are. If you find the number of trades too low despite a high win rate, you may loosen a few conditions to create a better balance.

So, we've now reached the end of the *Market Statistics* process. Remember, market statistics isn't just a record-keeping exercise — it's a deep process of refining your trading mindset. You're not only looking for an effective pattern; you're also building the ability to observe, analyze causes, and continuously improve your system.

After hundreds or even thousands of trades, you'll come to realize:

- Every losing trade is valuable data.
- Every obstacle has a reason behind it.

- Every refinement to your rules brings you one step closer to a trading system with stable, positive expectancy.

Backtesting

Once you've completed the market statistics phase, built your set of trading rules, and identified the setups with the highest probability, the next step is to test your system as if you were trading live — candle by candle. This is where we move into the *Backtesting* stage, an essential part of every serious trader's development journey.

Backtesting is not just about checking whether your system "works" or not. It's a complete test of your discipline, consistency, and adaptability to different market conditions. Just as a pilot must log hundreds of hours in a simulator before flying a real aircraft, a trader needs to "fly" their system in a simulated environment to ensure that every rule functions smoothly and reliably.

The Purpose of Backtesting

Backtesting allows you to:

- Measure the actual performance of your system using real market data.
- Determine the expected return and identify the maximum losing streak.
- Train your trading psychology and discipline — because during backtesting, you'll experience the same emotional rhythm of wins and losses as in live trading.
- And finally, build statistical confidence in your system.

Once you have that confidence, you'll no longer be shaken by short-term losing streaks. Instead, you'll understand that every drawdown or losing phase likely falls within the range of outcomes you've already tested and verified.

Professional Backtesting Tool - Forex Tester Online

To make your backtesting process truly effective, you need a specialized tool. Among the available options on the market, **Forex Tester Online** stands out as my favorite backtesting platform.

Forex Tester Online is a leading backtesting platform that brings your trading strategies to life with unparalleled realism and precision. It allows traders to simulate real market conditions, gain confidence in their methods, and refine their approach before risking actual capital.

Some of the features that make Forex Tester Online the gold standard for backtesting include:

- **Real Tick-by-Tick Data:** Unlike most backtesting platforms that show only completed candlesticks, Forex Tester Online lets you observe every price movement inside each candle, giving a realistic feel of live market conditions.

- **23 Years of Market Data:** This extensive history allows you to backtest your strategy across bull, bear, and sideways markets, providing confidence that your approach works consistently over the long term.

- **Browser-Based Platform:** You can access your projects from any device with a browser, making it easy to continue practicing or analyzing your trades without being tied to a single computer.

- **Automated Trading and Expert Advisors:** Whether you prefer discretionary trading or algorithmic strategies, you can simulate them side by side to find the optimal combination and improve overall performance.

- **Advanced Position Management**: With Forex Tester Online, you can instantly jump to your take profit or stop loss levels, monitor trades in real time, and adjust the speed of the market simulation as needed. It also allows you to set stop-loss levels either as a fixed dollar amount or as a percentage of your account, helping you maintain consistent and precise risk management across all trades.

- **Analytics and Performance Insights:** The platform generates detailed statistics on your trades, enabling you to evaluate your strengths and weaknesses and providing actionable insights to help you improve continuously.

- **MT4/MT5 Trade Import:** You can upload your past trades from other platforms and instantly backtest them, gaining a clear understanding of your real performance patterns without guesswork.

- **Prop Firm Challenge Simulation:** You can simulate real prop firm funding challenges or create custom challenges to test your strategy under strict rules, daily loss limits, and drawdown constraints, ensuring your approach is fully prepared for funded trading environments.

These are only a few of the platform's standout features—there's so much more that makes it truly exceptional. The best way to experience all its powerful capabilities is to try it yourself and see the difference.

With Forex Tester Online, you can backtest not just the breakout strategy but any trading method, anytime, anywhere. Start exploring its powerful tools now via **shorturl.at/BmOL9**.

Step-by-Step Backtesting Process

To get the most out of Forex Tester, you can follow this structured workflow:

Step 1: Prepare your data and chart setup

- Choose the currency pair or asset you usually trade.
- Select a timeframe that matches your trading style (D1, H4, M15, etc.).
- Pick a point in the past from which to start your backtest.

Step 2: Simulate Your Trades

- Use the complete set of rules you refined during the Market Statistics phase — follow them closely and with full discipline.
- Let the price play forward candle by candle or in segments, depending on your preferred pace.
- When a valid breakout pattern appears and all conditions are met, execute the trade exactly according to your rules.

Step 3: Evaluate Your Results

After completing a sufficient number of trades (at least 100), open the analytics panel at the bottom right corner of the trading platform. There, you'll find a wealth of metrics on your past trades—insights that might surprise you. I won't reveal all of them here; it's something you have to experience yourself to fully appreciate the thrill of analyzing your trades with Forex Tester Online.

Step 4: Review and Refine

- Take detailed notes on the factors that commonly lead to losing trades.

- Remove or adjust any elements that consistently reduce performance or lower probability.

- Repeat the backtesting process after making refinements to confirm whether your adjustments have truly improved the system's overall results.

When to End Your Backtesting

Backtesting isn't something you do just once and move on. It's a recurring process — one that should be repeated regularly, especially whenever you update or expand your trading system. Each time you adjust your rules, you should backtest at least 100 trades to make sure those changes don't negatively affect your system's overall performance.

As you backtest over time, you'll begin to develop what I call *data-based confidence* — the kind of confidence that comes from numbers, not emotions. You'll know:

- When your system performs best,

- When to stay out of the market, and,

- When facing a losing streak, where your safety threshold lies — when to stop before things get worse.

That's the moment you're ready to move on to the next critical part of your journey: **Risk Management.**

Backtesting helps you identify whether your system truly has a statistical edge. But that edge only matters if you know how to protect it. If *Market Statistics* and *Backtesting* teach you how much the market can give you, then *Risk Management* teaches you how much you can afford to lose and still survive long enough to see your strategy prove itself in the real market.

In the next section, we'll build a **three-layer risk management framework — 1% / 5% / 20%** — a solid protection system designed to help you stay in the game long enough to let your strategy's edge fully unfold.

Risk Management

Once you've completed your backtesting and confirmed that your system truly has a statistical edge, your trading journey doesn't end there. A system may be profitable, but without proper risk management, it can still lead to a blown account.

The market never moves perfectly. There will be days when price moves against your analysis, unexpected losing streaks, and even periods when you trade flawlessly yet still face disappointing results. During those times, risk management is your shield — it protects you and allows you to stay in the game long enough for your system's edge to show its real power.

Just as an architect doesn't focus solely on creating a beautiful design but also ensures that the building can withstand storms, a trader must have a solid risk management framework to safeguard everything they've built.

We'll now construct a three-layer risk management system, consisting of:

- 1% maximum risk per trade,
- 5% maximum daily loss limit, and
- 20% maximum overall drawdown for the entire account.

These are not just dry numbers — they are *three layers of survival protection*, helping you trade with discipline, stay emotionally stable, and preserve your system's long-term statistical advantage.

First Layer - Maximum Risk per Trade: 1% of Account

This is the first and most important principle of risk management: every trade you take must not risk more than 1% of your total account balance, calculated based on the distance between your entry point and your stop loss.

For example:

- Account size: $100,000 → maximum risk per trade = $1,000.
- If your stop loss is 20 pips away, each pip should be worth $50.
- That means your position size should be adjusted so that your total risk stays within the $1,000 limit.

This rule protects your ability to recover. Even if you lose five trades in a row, your total loss is only 5% of your account — still within a safe range that allows you to stay calm and continue trading systematically.

Remember:

A good trader doesn't try to avoid losses — they make sure every loss is small and under control.

Second Layer - Daily Maximum Loss: 5%

The second layer of protection is your *Daily Maximum Loss* (DML) — the limit on how much you're allowed to lose in a single day.

A 5% limit acts as a circuit breaker that stops you before emotions take over rational thinking.

For example, if you have a $100,000 account, a 5% DML means your daily stop-loss threshold is $5,000. If you lose five consecutive trades (each risking 1% of your account), you must stop trading immediately — no matter how promising the market may seem afterward.

This rule protects not only your capital but also your mindset. After a series of consecutive losses, your ability to make sound decisions is often distorted — you start looking for "revenge trades," acting on emotion rather than logic, and digging yourself into deeper losses.

Stopping once you hit the 5% daily loss limit helps you maintain discipline and mental clarity, ensuring that you can return to the market the next day with a clear head and renewed focus.

Third Layer - Maximum Overall Drawdown: 20%

The final layer of protection is your *Maximum Drawdown (MDD)* — the largest overall decline you allow on your entire account. This acts as the emergency brake of your risk management system.

With an MDD limit of 20%, you will temporarily stop trading if your account drops from $100,000 to $80,000. At that point, your goal is not to recover the losses immediately, but to reassess your entire system:

- Have you deviated from your trading rules?
- Are your entry conditions still aligned with the current market environment?
- Do you need to adjust your trade frequency or refine your setup filters?

The MDD rule prevents catastrophic losses from occurring. A trader who loses 20% can recover, but a trader who loses 50% must double their account — a 100% gain — just to break even, which is nearly impossible in the short term.

That's why a 20% MDD limit is considered the survival threshold — the line that keeps you in the game long enough to build a sustainable trading career.

Three Layers - One Complete System

These three limits form a complete and self-contained risk management framework, where each layer serves as an independent yet interconnected level of protection:

Layer	Limit	Objective	Main Function
Single Trade	1%	Control risk per trade	Reduce the impact of individual mistakes
Daily Loss	5%	Cap daily drawdown	Prevent losing streaks from spiraling and protect your psychology
Total Account	20%	Limit overall drawdown	Ensure long-term safety and prevent capital collapse

With these three protective layers in place, you maintain control over losses at every level — from individual trades to full trading cycles. Even during temporary drawdown periods, this system ensures you have both the capital and the mental resilience to recover and return to the market.

The "Defensive First" Mindset - Winning Through Survival

One of the biggest differences between amateur and professional traders lies in how they perceive risk. Beginners often focus on "how to make as much profit as possible." Professionals, on the other hand, ask themselves:

"If everything goes wrong, how much will I lose — and can I live with that?"

This *defense-before-offense* mindset is what allows them to stay in the game long enough to succeed. Because in trading, you don't need to win every battle — you just need to avoid being knocked out of the game.

The three numbers — 1%, 5%, and 20% — may seem small, but they form the foundation of every professional trader's survival strategy. Once you master these limits, you stop gambling with the market and start managing your own risk with intention and control.

Think of your capital as oxygen — once you lose it, everything else stops. A solid trading system must be built on a strong foundation of capital protection:

- 1% protects every small breath,
- 5% protects your mental clarity each day,
- 20% protects your entire trading career.

After going through this entire chapter — from Market Statistics and Backtesting to Risk Management — you now hold the three essential pillars that turn a trading strategy from theory into a system that can truly operate and generate profit in the real market.

Market Statistics teaches you to see the market through data — to understand how effective your method really is and under what conditions it performs best. Backtesting allows you to test those insights in real historical conditions, trade by trade and setup by setup, thereby gaining a deeper understanding of how the market reacts to your rules. And finally, Risk Management serves as your shield — protecting you through losing streaks, maximizing winning phases, and preserving the stability you need to grow in an ever-changing market.

Many traders fail not because their methods are bad, but because they lack the patience to validate them, or the discipline to manage risk correctly. When you know your method's true win rate, its average R:R, and its maximum drawdown — and still maintain consistency in execution — that's when trading stops being a game of luck and becomes a game of probability, structure, and control.

THE SNIPER'S WAY

So, we've reached the final chapter of this book. And in this closing section, I'd like to invite you to look back at everything we've learned — but from a very different perspective: **the perspective of a sniper.**

You've probably heard the phrase *"trade like a sniper"* countless times. And maybe, like many others, you've thought it meant taking very few trades — waiting patiently for only the most perfect setups, maybe one or two trades a week, or even just a few per month. Because of that, many traders assume *sniper trading* means sitting on the daily or 4-hour chart, waiting endlessly for the "perfect shot."

But that's not really the essence of it. To *trade like a sniper* has little to do with your timeframe, trade frequency, or how long you hold a position. It has everything to do with **your mindset, your process, and your discipline.**

A sniper doesn't shoot less because he's afraid of missing — he shoots less because he knows exactly *when not to pull the trigger.* He understands that every bullet counts, and that precision matters far more than volume. He only takes the shot when all the variables align — when the environment, the distance, the wind, and the target all come together to create the highest probability of success.

Before we go any further, let's take a closer look at what a real sniper represents — because through that image, we'll begin to see why the mindset of a sniper holds so many valuable lessons for traders.

When we think of a sniper, we often picture someone lying perfectly still, one eye pressed to the scope, breath calm and steady, waiting for the one perfect moment to pull the trigger. They embody patience, precision, and absolute control — not just of their weapon, but of their mind and body under extreme conditions. And when they finally take the shot, it lands exactly where it's meant to.

In many ways, a true trader is just like that. Patient. Composed. Precise.

In trading, the market is not your enemy — it's simply the battlefield. As traders, we're just a small part of that vast environment. We can't control the market's movement, but we can control ourselves. Your trading strategy is your weapon, and just like a sniper's rifle, it's only as effective as the skill of the person using it.

Unfortunately, many traders do the exact opposite. They step onto the financial battlefield without a weapon — or worse, with too many of them. They collect countless strategies, indicators, and systems, but never master any single one.

Before a sniper ever steps onto the battlefield, they spend thousands of hours in training. They fire dozens of rounds every day, thousands each month — not because they enjoy it, but because they *must* in order to turn their reflexes into instinct.

Now imagine if that sniper only fired two or three bullets a week — could they ever become truly elite? Of course not. The same principle applies to trading. You can't expect mastery if you only "pull the trigger" two or three times a week and hope for great results. Every skill — whether it's marksmanship or trading — is built on consistent, deliberate practice, repeated day after day until precision becomes second nature.

A skilled sniper never stops training, even after reaching mastery. They keep sharpening their craft so that their edge never dulls. Take Simo Häyhä, the legendary Finnish sniper of World War II, who recorded over 500 confirmed kills in just 100 days — an average of five per day. He didn't shoot *less* — he shot *accurately.*

And that's the essence of trading. The question isn't whether you trade often or rarely, or whether you prefer higher or lower timeframes. The real question is: *how precise are your shots?*

A great trader can identify high-probability entries in any timeframe. What makes you a "sniper trader" is not the chart you use — it's your mindset and discipline. Can you stay calm enough to wait for a truly clean setup? Can you pull the trigger at exactly the right moment — no hesitation, no doubt? And most importantly, have you trained enough to know when *not* to shoot?

Just like a sniper, a trader must train every single day. While you only take a few trades per week in the live market, during your *Market Statistics* and *Backtesting* phases, you can practice dozens or even hundreds of trades a day. The more you practice, the clearer your understanding becomes: which setups tend to win, which ones tend to fail, and what rules you need to refine to improve your edge. That's the beauty of Market Statistics and Backtesting — they let you train endlessly, without ever running out of bullets.

And just like a sniper, when you step onto the real battlefield, you fight alone. During training, you might have mentors or teammates to correct your mistakes. But when you face the market, *you* are the one who must pull the trigger.

Yet many traders make the mistake of outsourcing this responsibility — they follow signal groups, copy trades, or depend on others to tell them when to enter and exit. But when you don't aim and pull the trigger yourself, you're no longer a sniper — you're just someone taking orders.

Trading, like sniping, is not about shooting *more* or *less* — it's about precision and consistency.

Shooting rarely but missing still means nothing. True mastery comes from thousands of hours of focused, deliberate practice — from constantly refining your skill and maintaining razor-sharp focus no matter what the market throws at you. The market will never be under your control. The only thing you can truly control is *yourself*.

So if, by the time you've reached this point, this book has given you even a small insight — a single spark that helps you see trading differently — I'll be deeply grateful if you share your thoughts or leave a short review.

Because somewhere out there, another trader, just like you once were, might find a light for their own journey.

Finally, I wish you to become a true *sniper trader* — not because you take few trades, but because every shot you take is *calm, confident, and precise.*

If you ever have questions, insights, or simply want to share your journey, I'd be truly glad to hear from you. You can reach me anytime at tom.kenneth.anderton@gmail.com.